TOM CRUISE

TOM CRUISE

Phelan Powell

Introduction by James Scott Brady,
Trustee, the Center to Prevent Handgun Violence
Vice Chairman, the Brain Injury Foundation

Chelsea House Publishers
Philadelphia

Frontis: Tom Cruise's good looks and acting ability have won him both a worldwide following and numerous awards.

CHELSEA HOUSE PUBLISHERS

EDITOR IN CHIEF Stephen Reginald
PRODUCTION MANAGER Pamela Loos
MANAGING EDITOR James D. Gallagher
DIRECTOR OF PHOTOGRAPHY Judy L. Hasday
ART DIRECTOR Sara Davis
SENIOR PRODUCTION EDITOR Lisa Chippendale

Staff for **Tom Cruise**
ASSOCIATE ART DIRECTOR Takeshi Takahashi
DESIGNER 21st Century Publishing and Communications, Inc.
PICTURE RESEARCHER Patricia Burns
COVER ILLUSTRATION Cliff Spohn
COVER DESIGN Brian Wible

First Printing

1 3 5 7 9 8 6 4 2

Library of Congress Cataloging-in-Publication Data

Powell, Phelan.
Tom Cruise / Phelan Powell.
110 p.   cm. — (Overcoming Adversity)
Includes bibliographical references and index.
Summary: Follows the life and career of the popular actor, focusing on his struggle with dyslexia, his starring roles in such movies as "Risky Business," "Top Gun," and "Jerry Maguire," and his involvement in the Church of Scientology.
ISBN 0-7910-4940-X (hardcover) — ISBN 0-7910-4941-8 (pbk.)
1. Cruise, Tom, 1962–   —Juvenile literature. 2. Motion picture actors and actresses—United States—Biography—Juvenile literature. [1. Cruise, Tom, 1962–   . 2. Actors and actresses.] I. Title. II. Series.
PN2287.C685P68   1999
791.43'028'092—dc21
[B]   98–47621
                                                          CIP
                                                          AC

CONTENTS

OVERCOMING ADVERSITY

TIM ALLEN
comedian/performer

MAYA ANGELOU
author

DREW CAREY
comedian/performer

JIM CARREY
comedian/performer

BILL CLINTON
U.S. President

TOM CRUISE
actor

WHOOPI GOLDBERG
comedian/performer

EKATERINA GORDEEVA
figure skater

SCOTT HAMILTON
figure skater

JAMES EARL JONES
actor

ABRAHAM LINCOLN
U.S. President

WILLIAM PENN
Pennsylvania's founder

ROSEANNE
entertainer

ON FACING ADVERSITY

James Scott Brady

I GUESS IT'S a long way from a Centralia, Illinois, train yard to the George Washington University Hospital Trauma Unit. My dad was a yardmaster for the old Chicago, Burlington & Quincy Railroad. As a child, I used to get to sit in the engineer's lap and imagine what it was like to drive that train. I guess I always have liked being in the "driver's seat."

Years later, however, my interest turned from driving trains to driving campaigns. In 1979, former Texas governor John Connally hired me as a press secretary in his campaign for the American presidency. We lost the Republican primary to a former Hollywood star named Ronald Reagan. But I managed to jump over to the Reagan campaign. When Reagan was elected in 1980, I was "sitting in the catbird seat," as humorist James Thurber would say—poised to be named presidential press secretary. I held that title throughout the eight years of the Reagan administration. But not without one terrible, extended interruption.

It happened barely two months after the Reagan administration took office. I never even heard the shots. On March 30, 1981, my life went blank in an instant. In an attempt to assassinate President Reagan, John Hinckley Jr. armed himself with a "Saturday night special"—a low-quality, $29 pistol—and shot wildly as our presidential entourage exited a Washington hotel. One of the exploding bullets struck me just above the left eye. It shattered into a couple dozen fragments, some of which penetrated my skull and entered my brain.

The next few months of my life were a nightmare of repeated surgery, broken contact with the outside world, and a variety of medical complications. More than once, I was very close to death.

The next few years were filled with frustrating struggles to function with a paralyzed right side, struggles to speak and communicate.

To people who face and defeat daunting obstacles, "ambition" is not becoming wealthy or famous or winning elections or awards. Words like "ambition" and "achievement" and "success" take on very different meanings. The objective is just to live, to wake up every morning. The goals are not lofty; they are very ordinary.

My own heroes are ordinary folks—but they accomplish extraordinary things because they try. My greatest hero is my wife, Sarah. She's accomplished a lot of things in life, but two stand out. The first has been the way she has cared for me and our son since I was shot. A tremendous tragedy and burden was dropped unexpectedly into her life, totally beyond her control and without justification. She could have given up; instead, she focused her energies on preserving our family and returning our lives to normal as much as possible. Week by week, month by month, year by year, she has not reached for the miraculous, just for the normal. Yet in focusing on the normal, she has helped accomplish the miraculous.

Her other most remarkable accomplishment, to me, has been spearheading the effort to keep guns out of the hands of criminals and children in America. Opponents call her a "gun grabber"; I call her a national hero. And I am not alone.

After a seven-year battle, during which Sarah and I worked tirelessly to educate the public about the need for stronger gun laws, the Brady Bill became law in 1993. It was a victory, achieved in the face of tremendous opposition, that now benefits all Americans. From the time the law took effect through fall 1997, background checks had stopped 173,000 criminals and other high-risk purchasers from buying handguns, and the law has helped to reduce illegal gun trafficking.

Sarah was not pursuing fame, or even recognition. She simply started at one point—when our son, Scott, found a loaded handgun on the seat of a pickup truck and, thinking it was a toy, pointed it at Sarah.

Fortunately, no one was hurt. But seeing a gun nearly bring a second tragedy upon our family, Sarah became determined to do whatever she could to prevent senseless death and injury from guns.

Some people think of Sarah as a powerful political force. To me, she's the person who so many times fed me and helped me dress during my long years of recovery.

Overcoming obstacles is part of life, not just for people who are challenged by disabilities, illnesses, or tragedies, but for all people. No matter what the obstacle—fear, disability, prejudice, grief, or a difficulty that isn't likely to "just go away"—we can all work to make this world a better place.

Cruise, playing cocky pilot Pete "Maverick" Mitchell, straps himself into a fighter jet. Fueled by the success of Top Gun, *his film career was about to take off beyond his wildest dreams.*

1

FLYING HIGH

THE MILLIONS OF moviegoers who watched the action film *Top Gun*, about the U.S. Navy's training school for its best aviators, saw pilot Pete "Maverick" Mitchell, a young man with talent and ambition, struggle with inner demons. Many viewers who watched the movie in the summer of 1986 loved the action sequences on the aircraft carrier, vicariously placing themselves in the cockpit of a navy F-14 fighter jet. Other moviegoers flocked to the film to enjoy the romance between Kelly McGillis and the handsome and cocky pilot.

Top Gun's Maverick is a reckless but skilled pilot—perhaps the best in his class at the navy's Miramar training school for its "top guns." But he is troubled by unresolved questions about the death of his father, also a navy pilot, and haunted by the death of his best friend and copilot, nicknamed "Goose," in an accident caused by Maverick's aggressive flying. After the accident, Maverick questions himself and nearly loses his nerve to fly, but he overcomes his fear during a heroic, nail-biting aerial duel with Russian MIG fighter jets. After the triumphant battle with the enemy, in which Maverick is forced to control

*Tom Cruise and Nicole Kidman are among the most popular and powerful couples in Hollywood.
Both big-name stars, the two also share a rewarding personal life with their two adopted children,
Connor and Isabella.*

both his fear and his emotions, his reputation among his peers soars meteorically.

The role of Maverick did the same thing for Tom Cruise's career, launching the actor high into the rarefied stratosphere of box office stardom. *Top Gun* parallels Cruise's life in other ways as well. The actor, born Thomas Cruise Mapother IV, endured a troubled, itinerant, and often fatherless youth, and struggled with an undiagnosed learning disorder called dyslexia. These problems made life frustrating for the young Cruise. In 1998 he told *A&E Biography Magazine*, "I was always in remedial reading class. It was very embarrassing." Despite these troubles, he was able to control his fears and harness his talent, as Maverick does in *Top Gun*, to become one of the best-known actors in the world. *Entertainment Weekly* has called Tom "the most successful film star of his generation," and *People* has noted, "If you just met him and talked to him for 15 seconds, maybe just said hello or shook hands, you'd feel you'd had an experience."

Cruise has successfully overcome both his childhood traumas and his learning disorder to achieve greatness as an actor. In 1985 he was invited to a White House ceremony that honored him with an award for Outstanding Learning Disabled Achievement. By that time he had starred in six films, an accomplishment that demonstrated he had not allowed his dyslexia to be a barrier to success.

Cruise has matched his flourishing career with a happy family. He and Australian actress Nicole Kidman make up one of Hollywood's "power couples," and they are raising two adopted children, Isabella and Connor. Having learned a lesson from his own childhood—how hard it is for a child to have a father continuously immersed in his work instead of his family—Tinseltown's biggest box-office star often brings his children with him onto movie sets. Cruise once showed up at a script development meeting with baby Connor bundled into a Snugli.

The actor is also a genuinely nice person. In March 1996 he saw a young woman get hit by a speeding car on Wilshire Boulevard in Santa Monica. He went with her to the hospital, and when he learned that she had no health insurance, he paid her $7,000 medical bill. When he saw two young boys being crushed by surging crowds at the London premier of his film *Mission: Impossible*, he pulled them out of the mob to safety. In August 1996, while yachting off the island of Capri, he sent his skiff to rescue passengers from a sailboat that caught fire nearby. The five passengers were taken off their boat just minutes before it sank. And in October 1998 he and his body-guards chased away a group of muggers who had attacked one of his London neighbors, Rita Simmonds.

His fine-tuned focus has given Cruise a reputation for being a hard worker on the set. No matter how strong or weak a script might prove to be, he gives his best effort, and audiences continue to support him with their presence in theaters around the world whenever his name is the headliner. He is a man who seems to be in perfect control of himself at all times. "I'm still reckless, but in a more specific way," Tom admits when discussing his life before stardom. "My recklessness goes through to my work. I was always looking for attention. I'd get into fights. I think it was out of a need to be creative, because if you can't create, you eventually start to destroy yourself."

Tom Cruise has always decried the emphasis on his looks as the key to his success, but there is no denying that many women of all ages need nothing more than a passing glance at his bright white smile and intense eyes to send their hearts into spasms of love arrhythmia. Why else would a woman like talk show host Rosie O'Donnell, who is in her thirties and the mother of an adopted son and daughter, go absolutely gaga when Tom was a guest on her show? She unabashedly claimed she was "all tingly with excitement" at the prospect of meeting her screen idol and even had a towel nearby to dry palms sweaty from nervousness.

Tom Cruise responded to O'Donnell's over-the-top adoration with his typical charm and humility. In fact, his humility was noted in the November 17, 1997, issue of *People*. The magazine, which has named Cruise one of the "50 Most Beautiful People" on three different occasions, ran a feature entitled "Face-off: How Today's Heartthrobs Compare with Generations Past," in which Tom Cruise was compared with Clark Gable, known in the 1930s as the King of Hollywood. "Their most endearing quality, though, is humility," *People* reported. In the article, director Rob Reiner said of Tom: "He forgets he's a star. He just goes along like a normal person."

It seems that every movie this "normal person" makes becomes a box-office hit, simply because the name "Tom Cruise" heads the credits.

Tom Cruise, shortly after high school. Because he suffered from the learning disorder dyslexia, which affected his reading, spelling, and writing skills, school was torturous. Cruise now sees this difficult period of his life as a "character-building stage."

2

FROM FAR AND AWAY

DILLON HENRY MAPOTHER could not have known what lay ahead when he set off from Ireland on a great adventure almost 150 years ago. Dillon must have spent many an hour gazing over the rough ocean whitecaps on his long voyage to America. It was 1850, and Ireland was in the throes of a terrible famine. Prospects for any sort of good life there were dim indeed. The promise of a future in the country called America filled his heart and spirit with hope, so he stood on the ship's deck, dreaming of the land that lay beyond the frothy waves.

Dillon made the long and dangerous voyage because he believed he and his descendants would have a better-than-even chance to make a good living in the faraway country. But nowhere in his wildest imaginings could he have dreamed that 140 years later, one of his descendants would be among the world's most famous actors. Dillon would have thought the air was thick with the mischief of leprechauns if someone had told him that Thomas Cruise Mapother IV would return to Ireland and be paid $12 million to make the film *Far and Away* in 1991.

In fact, as Dillon was making his voyage, the motion picture industry was little more than a concept. In 1832 a Belgian inventor named Joseph Plateau had built an early projector called a *phenakistoscope*. Making use of a natural phenomenon known as "persistence of vision," in which the eye fills in missing motion between successive still drawings, this device used rotating disks, drawings, and a mirror to produce moving images. Two years later a similar invention, called the *zoetrope*, was made by William G. Horner. The zoetrope, which was sold in stores as a toy, used images attached to a revolving drum to depict motion. Inventor Thomas Edison, who developed the basic film projector that is still used today, was only three years old as Dillon's ship cut through the waves of the Atlantic Ocean.

Dillon Mapother was a surveyor by trade, and he decided to make his home in Louisville, Kentucky, a bustling river port and railroad hub. By 1850 the city was one of the most important industrial, financial, and shipping centers in the South, and n illions of immigrants intent on settling in the new land came through Louisville as America pushed its frontiers westward.

Dillon soon settled into his new home. Before his first year in America was over, he had courted and married a pretty woman named Mary Cruise. The Mapothers had two sons, Dillon and Wible, and became a respected family in Louisville society. The happy, stable family sustained a terrible blow in the mid-1870s when Dillon Sr. died suddenly of food poisoning and Mary found herself left to raise the family on her own. Mary rose to the challenge by taking on part-time jobs in order to feed her two youngsters and keep a roof over their heads.

Fortunately she was not alone for long, for the strong and attractive woman met and married another Irishman within a year of Dillon's death. Mary took his family name, O'Mara, as her own, but when she gave birth

to their son on December 29, 1876, the baby was inexplicably given her first husband's last name: Thomas Cruise Mapother. This curious event has caused many members of the Louisville Mapothers to believe they are not directly related to Tom Cruise's side of the family.

Little is known about Mary's son Dillon's accomplishments, but Wible, who had begun his employment as an office boy, became the youngest president ever of the Louisville and Nashville Railroad. As befitted such an

Making the 1991 film Far and Away *was particularly rewarding for Cruise because of his ancestral link to Ireland. His own great-great-grandfather, Dillon Henry Mapother, had left the country during a famine in 1850 to come to America.*

accomplishment, Wible lived in an exquisite mansion in the finest section of the city. Mary's youngest child was no slouch, either, when it came to ambition. Perhaps Wible's energetic success as well as Mary's constant encouragement were the propellants that shot Thomas through law school to become one of Louisville's youngest lawyers and, eventually, a Jefferson County Court judge. A few years after he began practicing law, Thomas married Anna Stewart Batman. By 1908 they had become a family of four with the births of sons Paul and Thomas Cruise Mapother II.

The elder Thomas saw his son and namesake also choose law as a career and successfully pass through the University of Louisville and the Jefferson School of Law. Thomas Mapother happily attended his son's wedding and lived long enough to see the birth of his grandchildren Thomas Cruise III in 1934 and William in 1938. The proud grandfather died a year later at the age of 62 while on a walk with his son Thomas and his wife, Anna.

William Mapother carried on what was by now a family tradition—entering the field of law. He, too, was a high achiever, becoming a judge by the age of 29. His brother, Thomas Cruise Mapother III, did not go into law. From an early age, he had been passionately curious about how things worked. He studied engineering, a field in which he excelled, at the University of Kentucky but diverted his fascination with technology long enough to marry a young woman named Mary Lee Pfeiffer. His bride was not from the Mapothers' level in Louisville society, however; her family came from the poorer section of town known as the Highlands. Nonetheless, the wedding was a joyous occasion celebrated by the members of both families.

After his marriage, Thomas took a position with General Electric as an engineer, a job that challenged his intellect. A workaholic by nature, Thomas was always more involved in his research than in his home life. This, sadly, would set the tone for his family relationships in the years to come. GE was attempting to develop new technologies, and this environment presented an intellectual paradise for someone like Tom Mapother, who could submerge himself in the excitement of his work: developing solid-state lasers.

The newlyweds were still living in Louisville when their first daughter, Lee Anne, was born. However, Thomas's job with GE soon forced the family to move to Syracuse, New York. This would be the first of many moves over the next two decades. While they were in Syracuse a second daughter, Marian, was born, followed by a son on July 3, 1962. The boy was named Thomas Cruise Mapother IV.

After a decade in the engineering field, Tom Mapother became obsessed with an idea: perhaps he could parlay his knowledge of laser research into an invention that would take the market by storm, thereby making him a rich man. The dozen years following his son's birth proved that Tom Mapother's marketing and business acumen was not in step with his scientific knowledge. Every 18 months or so the Mapothers uprooted house and home in order to follow the father's dreams of fame and fortune.

As Tom Mapother neglected his family in favor of his work, Mary Lee held the family—which had swelled to six with the birth of their third daughter, Cass—together with her energetic love and encouragement. Mary Lee had always been drawn to the theater and often, in a new town, she would make new acquaintances by joining a local performance company. As a result, all of her children were exposed to acting and the theater at a young age. Mary Lee used the theater as an outlet for her frustration with the family's constant moves.

Her son, however, had difficulties of his own, especially

A dyslexic student works on a writing exercise, illustrating the difficulty dyslexics have with transposing or reversing letters. "I was always in remedial reading class," Cruise recalled years later. "It was very embarrassing."

as he started school in Ottawa, Canada, where the Mapothers moved from Syracuse. Tom was the new kid on the block and had to make new friends. He knew how to ice skate pretty well, and that helped, but school was not his favorite place to be. His frustration with the move was compounded by his learning disorder. Like his mother and sisters, Tom was dyslexic.

Dyslexic is a term that is often used but is not well understood by the general public. The term comes from two Greek words: *dys* (difficulty) and *lexis* (words). A dyslexic literally has difficulty with words: reading, spelling, and writing. In addition, some 60 percent of

those diagnosed with dyslexia also have difficulty deal-
ing with numbers.

Dyslexics cannot look at a word and learn it in the
"normal" way. Children with dyslexia appear to have
severe problems with the simplest rules of language.
When a dyslexic looks at a word, he or she often sees it as
a hodgepodge of letters with no discernible shapes. For
example, the child may struggle with words such as "it"
and "the" or have trouble distinguishing between "from"
and "form." Unfortunately, children suffering from learning disorders are often labeled "dumb" by their peers,
even though their intelligence level may be higher than
average. The problem is that the child cannot learn in the
same way that other children do, because what he or she
sees makes no sense. Therefore, dyslexic children, whose
impairment can range from mild to severe, require early
identification and a suitable learning style in order to
negotiate their school years with some degree of success.
Even though early diagnosis can increase the likelihood of
academic success for many with the disorder, there is no
known cure for dyslexia or any other learning disorder. An
individual's success depends on the degree to which he or
she learns to compensate for his or her disability.

Researchers have determined that one person in 25 is
dyslexic. Dyslexia can be found among people of all
classes and intelligence levels. While the cause of
dyslexia is unknown, it is believed to be due to a combi-
nation of physiological, neurological, and genetic fac-
tors. Some studies indicate that a learning disorder can
result from the failure of one side of the brain to gain
dominance over the other side. In Tom Cruise's case, the
disorder appears to have been inherited.

As a child, Tom often found himself frustrated in his efforts
to succeed academically. "I had to train myself to focus my
attention," he said. "I became very visual and learned how to
create mental images in order to comprehend what I read."

Like Tom Cruise, Thomas A. Edison (1847–1931), one of the world's greatest inventors, was dyslexic. Although he died 30 years before Cruise was born, his work affected the future actor's career: Edison invented the first basic film projector, called a kinetoscope; it was the precursor of the modern-day movie camera.

Dyslexics often find themselves in the uncomfortable position of being sandwiched between their own perception of their world and the disappointment and disapproval of the authority figures around them. People with dyslexia are often highly creative but nevertheless suffer criticism. Others can see that the dyslexic student has a high level of talent, but what they may not realize is that his or her talent is coupled with a substantial inability to learn basic and standard material. Most people simply do not recognize or understand what dyslexics are going through.

Educators who study learning disabilities believe that

when a child's learning disorder is discovered, further study will often reveal a unique ability in the same individual. A roll call of famous dyslexics throughout the centuries, for example, includes the likes of Leonardo da Vinci and Michelangelo, British writer Agatha Christie, actors Henry Winkler, Whoopi Goldberg and Harry Anderson, pitching sensation Nolan Ryan, and perhaps the greatest mathematical genius of the century, Albert Einstein.

Tom Cruise also shares the disorder with the inventor who played a major part in the birth of the very film industry that has made Cruise a household name— Thomas Alva Edison. Speaking of his early days at school, Edison once said, "I remember I used to never be able to get along at school. I was always at the foot of the class. My father thought I was stupid, and I almost decided that I was a dunce."

A day in the life of a dyslexic youth is often filled with anxiety, which eventually leads to low self-esteem. Studies have found that normally achieving teenagers attribute their successes to their own abilities and their failures to something outside of themselves. Dyslexic adolescents, on the other hand, credit their successes to their hard work, but they blame their own lack of ability when they fail.

Tom Cruise was singled out as a slow learner in his early school years. Reading, spelling, and writing all confounded him as a youngster. Moving frequently from school to school did little to help the situation. Even though he was obviously struggling, teachers would often just shuttle him through the school year because they knew as well as Tom did that his stay in any one school system would be too short to be worth any intense expenditure of effort on their part. Fortunately his mother was versed in learning techniques that she could share with her children so their school experience would not be completely useless or disheartening. But academics were never enjoyable for Tom.

"It was tough because a lot of kids would make fun of me," Tom told an interviewer for *Today* in December 1994. "That experience made me very tough on the inside because you learn to quietly accept abuse and constant ridicule. . . . I now look on it as a character-building stage, although I hated every moment of my life in those days. I would come home crying so many times because of the misery of not being able to do as well in school as I knew I should be able to. . . . I had barriers to overcome. I was always put in remedial classes. I felt ashamed."

As an adult, Tom Cruise reveals relatively little about his childhood in interviews. Of his father he has said only that the senior Mapother was "complex, extremely bright, artistic." But perhaps any good times Tom shared with his father, who was nearly always working and on the move, were forever overshadowed the day in 1974 when his parents gathered the three girls and Tom in the living room. Tom's parents announced that their marriage was over and Tom's father was leaving the household for the last time. All the unkept promises, the moves, and the unending absences that had characterized their nearly 20 years of marriage had forced its dissolution.

The children were heartbroken. For a long time they had known that their parents were not as happy as they could be. But a broken home is never a child's choice, and the kids sat in the living room weeping. Tom's father took him outside to hit some baseballs around before he left. Was this a last-ditch attempt by the father to communicate the love he had for his son? Interestingly enough, many of the movies Tom Cruise has made depict him as a young man in quest of a paternal guide. Perhaps by playing such roles, he has experienced some of the satisfaction of the healthy father-son relationship that his own childhood lacked.

At the age of 12, Tom became the man of the house. He credits his mother and sisters with getting him through the

Tom's mother, Mary Lee Mapother (at left), held her family together with her energetic love and encour-
agement. Despite divorce and financial hardships, Mary taught Tom and his three sisters the value of
determination and hard work. "My mother is very giving, very open," Cruise said of her in later years.

difficult years immediately following the divorce. "My mother is very giving, very open," he said of her in later years. "She's a great listener. My sisters are very much like her: very strong women."

Without Thomas Mapother's income, however, the family was in financial trouble. But Mary Lee would not accept charity. She went to work, the girls worked as waitresses, and Tom delivered papers and cut lawns to help keep the family afloat financially.

Tom was very close to his sisters and learned through this closeness to appreciate all women. "Women to me are not a mystery," he once said in reply to a question about his sisters. "I get along easily with them." It is commonly understood among those who know him that he prefers the company of women to men. "I trust women easier than men," he has admitted.

In the year following the divorce, Tom and his family returned to the Louisville area, moving into a rented house in a lower-middle-class suburb. Tom became a loner. He attended St. Raphael's school and kept the details of his family's poverty hidden from his fellow students. When questioned, he would make up stories about a wonderful childhood.

After graduating from the eighth grade, Tom attended a seminary for a year. The school was located about 100 miles north of Louisville, near Cincinnati, Ohio. He received a scholarship to attend St. Francis Seminary for the 1976–77 school year, so it did not strain the family financially. Raised as a Roman Catholic, the teen considered the possibility of a vocation as a priest. At that time, the seminary school could boast that at least 25 percent of its graduating students entered the priesthood.

It was a hard year because it required being away from his beloved mother and sisters, but the school population was small and individual classroom attention, which Tom had long needed, was finally available. It was the best year Tom had ever had academically.

Tom had learned early on that one satisfactory outlet for the frustrations he experienced in the classroom was sports. He came to St. Francis already having learned to ski and skate, and at the school he played baseball, football, basketball, and lacrosse. St. Francis was a sports lover's paradise. Even though academics were stressed, the swimming pool, playing fields, tennis courts, and man-made lake provided great opportunities for the more than 100 students to explore their physical potential. Although Tom would never be an all-star, he was a good athlete.

Tom left the school after a year. It didn't take too many weekend sorties into town to meet girls for him to realize that he was not interested in becoming a priest. He returned to Louisville after his year at the seminary, but not to his mother's home. The family had moved out of their rented house because Mary Lee could no longer afford it, and they had moved in with Mary Lee's mother. The house was too small for Tom to live there as well, so he was sent to stay with his aunt and uncle on the other side of Louisville.

During the year Tom was in the seminary, there had been another big change in Mary Lee Mapother's life. She had met a man named Jack South who was strong and dependable, someone with whom she felt she could build a stable life. But Tom did not take to his mother's new love interest at all. He felt threatened; since her divorce, he had been the main man in her life.

Tom was unhappy living with his aunt and uncle, and Mary Lee was concerned about Tom's feelings toward Jack. Eventually she took another job and allowed Jack to help her financially. This meant Tom could come home to live with his family. Tom's feelings toward Jack South changed as he and his sisters realized how happy Jack made their mother. They noticed how well he treated her and agreed that their mother's happiness was something they all wanted to see after the years of hardship she had endured.

During high school, Cruise used his athletic ability and small size to his advantage by taking up wrestling. After an injury prevented him from continuing with the sport, he decided to give acting a try and landed a starring role in the school musical Guys and Dolls. *In this scene from* Born on the Fourth of July, *Tom gets to show off both of his high school talents.*

In 1977 Tom attended 10th grade at St. Xavier High School in Louisville. Mary Lee and Jack married the next spring and the entire family moved to Glen Ridge, New Jersey, a comfortable suburban town. Tom's stepfather rented a large clapboard house, and the six of them set about settling in and making friends in another new town. Tom attended Glen Ridge High School for his junior year, 1978–79, and joined the football team. Never a standout and small for his age at just 5′ 7″ and less than 150 pounds, Tom nonetheless gave the sport his best effort.

His lack of height contributed to his overall shyness as a teenager, particularly with girls. "Tom was real small," former girlfriend Nancy Armel said in a 1990 interview. "He was no heartthrob, that's for sure. He was a real nice guy, though, and great fun. He developed a great personality, really sincere." No doubt the strain of constantly moving from school to school during his childhood also contributed to his shyness.

After the football season ended, Tom decided to join the Glen Ridge High wrestling team. This was a sport in which his small size would not prevent him from excelling—wrestlers compete against others of approximately the same size and weight. Tom wrestled for the varsity team in the 115- or 122-pound weight classes.

It takes a long time to learn the moves and holds required to be a really good wrestler. In his first year Tom did not stand out among the 12 varsity wrestlers, but he worked hard to get better. Before one important match Tom had to lose a pound to make his weight class, and he decided to run up and down the stairs at home to lose the weight. Unfortunately, one of his sisters had left some school papers on the steps and Tom slipped on them, badly pulling the tendons in his knees. The injury ended his wrestling season, and Tom was left looking for a new way to release his pent-up energy.

As it turned out, the pulled tendons were probably a gift in disguise. That year Glen Ridge High was putting on *Guys and Dolls* as its annual school play. Now, unable to wrestle, Tom decided to try acting. His audition went well and he landed one of the musical's starring roles, Nathan Detroit, a hotshot gangster. Opening night was a glorious success. From that moment on, Tom Cruise knew exactly what he wanted to do with his life.

Cruise's first important film role was in Taps, *about a student uprising at a military academy. He is pictured here with costars Sean Penn and Timothy Hutton. Although he was initially selected for a small role, Cruise's ability caught the eye of the director, who decided he should be given a bigger part as a fanatical cadet who helps lead the revolt. The role won him critical praise but also briefly typecast Tom as an aggressive and violent character.*

3

PAYING HIS DUES

TOM ARRIVED HOME after his high school play's opening night with his head still echoing from the audience's applause.

A theater agent had watched his performance and came backstage to encourage what he called Tom's "natural talent." He advised the teenager to consider acting as a career. Tom was almost bouncing off the walls with enthusiasm later that evening as he told his mother and stepfather what he planned to do. He asked his family to allow him 10 years to see if he could make it as an actor. "I felt I needed to act the way I needed air to breathe," he later said of his feelings at that time.

Mary Lee saw her son's flair for acting as she proudly watched him perform on the stage. Jack South was skeptical of the boy's plans at first. But in the end, both gave him their blessing and support. After graduating from Glen Ridge High School in 1980, Thomas Cruise Mapother IV changed his name to Tom Cruise and set off for New York City.

The 17-year-old interviewed with an actor management agency, and his mother cosigned a five-year contract so he could audition for a candy commercial. The relationship with his new manager didn't work out, however. Tom ended up being a gofer for her, and he quickly terminated the agreement. He signed with another agent and began the daily grind of a typical actor-to-be in New York City: he went to auditions during the day, waited tables to earn extra cash between acting jobs, took classes to improve his acting skills, and tried to make his money stretch as far as possible.

Before long, Tom had an audition for a part in a movie that would be directed by Franco Zeffirelli, who had received acclaim for his films, including *Romeo and Juliet* (1968). This film, *Endless Love*, was based on a novel by Scott Spencer about two unhappy teenagers who fall dangerously and obsessively in love. The movie would feature 16-year-old Brooke Shields, a young star who had appeared in seven films and several provocative Calvin Klein jeans commercials. Martin Hewitt played the male lead, and Tom earned a small role as his pal Billy, a fun-loving jock who is light, airy, and animated compared to his depressed and sullen best friend.

It was a tiny beginning for the young star, but a beginning nonetheless. Although the movie was panned—one reviewer called it "a textbook example of how to do everything wrong in a literary adaptation"—Tom had little to do with the failure of the film, and his reputation was not affected.

Following his film debut, Tom returned to the real-life role of a struggling young actor in the big city. To save housing expenses, he took a job as superintendent of an apartment building. He was called on all hours of the day and night to resolve tenant complaints. Between auditions, waiting tables, and acting classes, Tom attended local performances to understand better the chemistry involved in successful stage performances. His cash was dwindling rapidly, but he hung on to the promise of that big break awaiting him just around the next corner.

It came in May 1981, in the form of a phone call from his agent, who wanted him to audition for a part in the movie *Taps*. Tom successfully breezed through the audition and was selected for a very minor role as a friend to one of the major characters. He soon met the rest of the cast, which included leading actors Sean Penn and Timothy Hutton, as filming began at the Valley Forge Military Academy near Philadelphia.

Taps is about a group of students at a venerated military academy. When the students learn that the school will be closed and razed to the ground so that a condominium development can be built in its place, they arm themselves and take over the buildings. The uprising results in the intervention of police and the military, and fails tragically in the end.

At director Harold Becker's insistence, all the actors cast as students lived the rigorous lifestyle of a student at a military academy. Tom lifted weights to put on 15 pounds of muscle to make his character more realistic. "I felt like it was a chance for me and a beginning," he said later. "We were really scared and nervous and excited. We didn't know what was going to happen. It was a special time in my life."

His intensity during the early days of shooting caught the eye of the director, who soon decided that Cruise should have a larger part in the movie. He was offered the role of David Shawn, a fanatical cadet leader of the uprising. "While we were in rehearsal I began to notice Tom," Becker recalled. "He became the character and just blew me away with his intensity. So I replaced one of the leading actors with him. It's what I call a battle-field promotion."

As filming progressed, Tom found common motivation in his character, who is loud, aggressive, and pugnacious. "A lot of that character was my childhood," he reflected. "I wasn't intense like that but the character is just fear. That's what he does when he's afraid. He fights." Unfortunately, by the time the filming ended Tom had so immersed himself in the antisocial lifestyle of his fictitious character that no one could stand to be around him. He finally had to take himself to a secluded retreat in southern Kentucky in order to rid himself of the negative aggressiveness of his screen role. In a 1986 *Rolling Stone* interview Penn characterized Tom's performance as "very intense, 200 percent there. It was overpowering."

Although *Taps* received mixed reviews, overall Hutton, Penn, and Cruise garnered praise for their performances. Financially the film was a success, pulling in $20.5 million at the box office. And his role in *Taps* had taught Tom Cruise one thing for sure: he was no longer interested in auditioning for television shows or commercials; he wanted a career in movies. However, he didn't want to be typecast as a maniacal killer, so he turned down a number of roles that were similar to David Shawn, aggressive and violent. "I wanted something that would be in sharp contrast to the brutal cadet in *Taps*," Tom said.

As a result, the next role he took was nothing like his previous one. Unfortunately, the experience was not as pleasant, either. In fact, Tom later called it "the most depressing experience of my life." Shortly after finishing the filming of *Taps*, he agreed to a part in the movie *Losin' It*, about four high school seniors who travel to Mexico for a wild weekend. While there, they meet a woman named Kathy, who is seeking a quickie divorce in Tijuana. The movie was supposed to be a funny look at a young man attempting to lose his virginity; instead,

Purposely looking to play a character different from Taps' *David Shawn, Cruise, shown here with costar Shelley Long, chose to play a high school senior in the coming-of-age comedy* Losin' It. *Unfortunately, the story was plotless and predictable. Tom used his negative experience in this film as a lesson to be more careful in choosing future projects.*

it was plotless and predictable. "You know you're in trouble when it's a comedy and everybody making the movie is miserable," Cruise commented later, adding:

> It was a real eye-opener. It made me understand how you really have to be careful . . . you've got to examine all the elements of a project. I learned a great lesson in doing that movie. I realized I'd have to learn how to survive in this business and not let it eat me up. I knew the kinds of films I wanted to work on from then on had to be made by the best people. . . . Money was never a factor with me—I wanted to learn on a film. Money goes, but what you learn can't be taken away from you. Even though the film wasn't as bad as it could have been, it still wasn't the kind I wanted to be involved with.

With the misery of *Losin' It* still fresh in his mind, Tom and his agent, Paula Wagner, began looking for his next project. He had first heard during Christmas 1981 that a film version of the short novel *The Outsiders* was being considered by legendary director Francis Ford Coppola. Cruise was immediately interested. *The Outsiders* had been one of the few books he had read and enjoyed in his youth. The story was set in Tulsa, Oklahoma, in the 1960s and was about the interaction of the town's social classes: the poor kids, nicknamed "Greasers," and the rich kids, nicknamed "Socs" (pronounced *so*-chez, short for socials).

Coppola was considered one of the greatest directors in the United States for his work on such films as *The Godfather* (1974) and *Apocalypse Now* (1979). Tom flew to Los Angeles to audition, and afterward, according to Wensley Clarkson's biography *Tom Cruise: Unauthorised*, told the director, "Look, I don't care what you give me. I really want to work with you. I want to be there on the set and watch. I'll do anything it takes;

I'll play any role in this." He was given the part of Steve Randle, one of the Greasers. By the time shooting began in March 1982, Coppola had assembled a cast of very talented young actors: Emilio Estevez, Rob Lowe, C. Thomas Howell, Matt Dillon, Ralph Macchio, Patrick Swayze, Leif Garrett, Diane Lane, and Tom Waits. "I took *The Outsiders* over a lot of other things," Tom later said. "It was a small role . . . but I was ecstatic to get that role because, at 19, I was going to work with Francis Ford Coppola."

Tom (right) took a small role as a "greaser" in 1982's The Outsiders *for the opportunity to work with legendary film director Francis Ford Coppola. He also got the chance to meet many young and talented actors, including (from left to right) Emilio Estevez, Rob Lowe, C. Thomas Howell, Matt Dillon, Ralph Macchio, and Patrick Swayze.*

S. E. Hinton, the author of *The Outsiders*, had worked with Coppola on the screenplay and had written very detailed notes on each character's background and motivation. Coppola, an advocate of method acting—a process by which actors prepare for their on-screen roles by living like the character offscreen—housed the actors who portrayed the rich Socs in a fancy hotel, while stowing Cruise and the other actors who played Greasers in tiny rooms, giving them little spending money. The director's aim was to create a natural antagonism between the actors that would translate to their screen performances. It worked. A pickup football game between the two groups of actors during a lull in shooting nearly ended in a bloodbath.

It was easy for Tom to play the part of a down-and-out kid from a broken home. Once again he found himself opening wounds from his past to express the emotions that he needed on the screen. He also had the cap removed from a tooth he had chipped in a childhood hockey match, and had a tattoo painted on his arm. Although he was relatively inexperienced, he was happy to be working with—and learning from—a great director and cast. "I remember feeling very good, building up confidence in my own instincts on acting," he later said. "And understanding more on each level; learning more about film acting and what I wanted to do."

All in all, *The Outsiders* was a good experience for Tom Cruise. Although the film opened to mixed reviews, it was very popular with its intended audience—teenagers, especially teen girls. Coppola's next project was based on another S. E. Hinton novel, *Rumble Fish*; he invited Cruise to continue working with him on this new film. Although he would have liked to do the film, Tom turned down the offer because he had already agreed to do another movie. He had no way of knowing what an impact this next film would have on his career.

At age 20, Cruise landed his first starring role, as Joel Goodsen in Risky Business. *The movie was a financial hit and firmly established Tom as a star.*

4

MAKING THE GRADE

"I GREW UP as a very competitive individual, and when you're at a constant disadvantage, you learn to do whatever it takes to succeed in life," Tom Cruise once said. That determination went into the pursuit of his next screen role. He had heard about a movie that a first-time director, Paul Brickman, was planning, called *Risky Business*. When Tom read the script, he was impressed—"I thought, finally, this is an intelligent, stylish piece of material," he later commented—and set about trying to get the leading role.

When the director learned that Cruise was interested in the role of Joel Goodson, a pampered preppy kid from the rich side of town, he remembered him as the young psycho from *Taps*. "This guy for Joel?" Brickman asked. "This guy is a killer! Let him do *Amityville 3*!" But after Cruise auditioned for the part the director was impressed and offered him the role—his first movie lead.

The female lead was played by Rebecca De Mornay. She was the same age as Cruise, but her childhood had been very different. She traveled through many foreign countries in her youth, sometimes attending school, sometimes not. Determined to become an actress, she moved to Los Angeles when she was in her late teens. *Risky Business* was her first major screen role.

Risky Business was written as a satire of 1980s materialism. The studio spent just $5.5 million to make the movie—a relatively small amount for the motion picture industry—but even before the film's release in August 1983, people felt it had the potential to be a big hit. *Risky Business* lived up to expectations: it grossed $63 million in the United States and audiences left theaters delighted with Tom Cruise's portrayal of Joel Goodson, who goes wild when his parents go out of town and leave him home alone.

A single image from the film probably did more for Tom Cruise's career than anything else before or since. Although originally just a line in the script and lasting only a minute in the film, the scene audiences remembered was Tom dancing to Bob Seger's classic song "Old Time Rock 'n Roll" while wearing a dress shirt, underwear, and socks, and lip-synching into a candlestick microphone. It was the funniest scene in the movie.

Another well-known image from *Risky Business* is a steamy love scene between Cruise and De Mornay that occurs on a train. Although they seemed to give off sparks on-screen, the love scene was work for the two actors. "I remember it was uncomfortable," Tom later said. "A love scene can really step over the line sometimes. I don't mean that I step over the line or that the other person steps over the line—it's just, how far do you go? And although it may be exciting and romantic for the audience—you hope it is, otherwise you're doing it for nothing—it's just kind of uncomfortable."

However, the actors did find themselves attracted to each other during the filming of *Risky Business*, and by the time the film was finished they were dating. Cruise's first celebrity relationship was rocky: the young couple in love were followed by celebrity photographers (called paparazzi) and were embarrassed by tabloid articles and magazine covers detailing the progress of their romance. They would remain together for a little more than a year, a long time by Hollywood standards. Tom, who doesn't like to talk about any aspect of his personal life,

While filming Risky Business, *Tom developed an off-screen romance with leading lady Rebecca De Mornay. It was the young actor's first brush with love in the spotlight, and the pair was constantly followed by reporters. Although they maintained their relationship for over a year, the two eventually parted.*

would not comment on his relationship with Rebecca for several years after their breakup. When he did finally allude to it, he said, "It wasn't like, 'Hey shake hands. It's been great, baby, let's have lunch.' When you care about someone that deeply it's always difficult, but it wasn't ugly."

Although his personal relationship with De Mornay didn't work out, Tom Cruise found that his career was finally taking off. The success of *Risky Business* made him a sought-after commodity for the first time. "I'd go into a meeting and have to work hard to make them seem interested, do my juggling act, prove myself to them," Tom said of his efforts to get parts before his big hit. "Now they say, 'I know he can do it.' They tell my agent, 'I'd like to meet him.'"

After *Risky Business*, Tom decided to take a movie role that would challenge him as a performer. He teamed up with Michael Chapman, a well-known cinematographer but first-time director, to make *All the Right Moves*. Tom was intrigued by the script about Stefan Djorjevic, a boy from a blue-collar family living in a struggling steel mill town in Pennsylvania. The character seeks to escape the inevitability of a hopeless future in a depressed steel town and fights to avoid the same leaden existence he sees his father and brother living. Djorjevic's ticket out of town is his athletic ability, so he works his heart out on the football field.

The story touched something deep inside Cruise:

There were times when my father was working. I remember that for about a year we lived in a nice house in a nice neighborhood. Then, later on, times got really tough. But it was exciting, challenging. And there was a sense of teamwork. We all worked together and when the team broke down, there were problems. It wasn't easy.

I think on certain levels I could identify with the guy, Stefan. But I didn't need the ticket out. I didn't feel that trapped. I was lucky enough to live in places where I could always make money.

Once again, Tom altered his appearance to fit the role—scrawny but muscular, hair dyed jet-black. He put himself out on the football field and took real hits, even receiving a mild concussion at one point. The movie was filmed in Johnstown, a depressed steel town in the

Cruise identified with his character in All the Right Moves: *a boy from a blue-collar family living in a depressed town. Stefan Djorjevic's athletic ability is his only hope to escape his bleak future. Tom lost weight, added muscle, and brushed up on his football game for the part. His hard work paid off in rave reviews by film critics.*

mountains of western Pennsylvania, where unemployment was nearly 25 percent. Tom was so touched by the townspeople he met and worked with on the film that he took out an ad in the local paper to express his thanks before he left.

Although *All the Right Moves* would never make a lot of money, Cruise was happy because the movie was well regarded critically. Nationally known film critic Roger Ebert called it "an astonishing breakthrough in movies about teenagers," and Kathleen Carroll of the *New York Daily News* wrote, "Tom Cruise is exceptionally appealing . . . . It is a gritty, dignified movie."

Just as he finished filming *All the Right Moves* Tom received word that his father, whom he hadn't seen in 10 years, was dying of cancer. After leaving his family, Tom Mapother had drifted, eventually remarrying. After splitting up with his second wife, he became sick and returned to Louisville, where his parents helped their down-and-out son rent a place to live. Cruise and his sisters visited their father before he died at age 50 on January 9, 1984, but Tom has never revealed his feelings about the reunion.

Shortly before his father's death, Tom decided to make *Legend* with director Ridley Scott. The film, about a quest to save a unicorn, was intended as a fairy-tale fantasy story for children. Unfortunately *Legend*'s beautiful, fantastic set was beset with delays and catastrophes both great (a fire burned the set down) and small (a fox Tom had to hold for many shots during filming scratched his arms badly).

The finished film was a disaster. After audiences previewed the trailer and laughed at Cruise in long hair and animal skins, studio executives seriously considered not releasing the film at all. It was released in the spring of

1986, and the Cruise name drew large enough crowds to make it the top-grossing film of its opening week. However, it quickly left theaters as the word spread: "Don't go see that film. It was awful."

"Making that movie was exhausting," Cruise later said, calling it "a torturous experience." Critics said that involvement with the flop would damage his career. But during the tedious shooting of *Legend*, Tom read the script that would send his popularity soaring beyond his wildest dreams.

Cruise received his star on the Hollywood Walk of Fame on Hollywood Boulevard in October of 1986, following his hits Risky Business *and* Top Gun. *The success of* Top Gun *made Tom the number-one box office star of the year.*

5

BECOMING A
TOP GUN

THE IDEA FOR *Top Gun* came from a magazine article about the U.S. Navy's school for fighter pilots. Writer Ehud Yonoy had taken an intensive look at the training ground for what were considered the navy's best fliers. The piece caught the attention of producer Jerry Bruckheimer and his partner Don Simpson, who immediately saw a story of action and drama featuring a hotshot navy aviator.

Bruckheimer and Simpson were already well-known producers, having collaborated on the megahits *Flashdance* and *Beverly Hills Cop*. Their movies combined action, sex, and music to appeal to a wide audience. The two worked on their story about competition in the sky and romance on the ground. As they researched their story, Bruckheimer and Simpson visited the Miramar Naval Air Station in San Diego, California, where they met many of the young, confident, athletic pilots they wanted to depict in the movie. Meeting the real-life pilots gave them an idea of the actor they wanted to cast as the lead in their movie. In Clarkson's *Tom Cruise: Unauthorised*, Bruckheimer recalled, "From the first time we went to Miramar, even before the script was written, we said, 'These guys are Tom Cruise.'"

Once the story was finished, they sold the rights to Paramount Pictures and then set about getting the navy's permission and assistance to make the movie. The producers knew they'd need to use the navy's equipment, especially the multimillion-dollar planes that were at the center of the story. Top navy brass realized that a film about military aviators could attract new recruits, and after the producers allowed the navy to review the script to ensure that the service would not be shown in an unfavorable light, Bruckheimer and Simpson received enthusiastic approval for the project. The navy offered practically unlimited use of facilities, planes, and personnel, provided the studio would assume the costs of using the equipment, such as $7,600 an hour for jet fuel. Paramount agreed.

With the project moving ahead, Simpson and Bruckheimer looked for a director. Coincidentally, they ended up selecting Tony Scott, the brother of Ridley Scott, with whom Cruise had just spent a miserable year making *Legend*. Tony didn't have any experience directing films, but he had developed a successful career directing television commercials, and he was excited about the story. "I jumped at the chance. Who wouldn't?" Scott commented later.

The producers gave Cruise a copy of the script early; in fact, he read it while working on *Legend*. He loved the story but felt that the script could be improved, and told Bruckheimer, Simpson, and Scott that he wanted input into rewriting the story. The three were skeptical, but they reluctantly agreed to hear Cruise out. Within a short time, they realized that Tom's suggestions had merit and would improve the final product. Tom wanted *Top Gun* to be a movie about characters and the human element of military life, not just a war picture, and he knew the focus should be on competition, not killing.

"I was against [Tom's altering the script] because I like to run things," Simpson said. "To me, an actor is generally a hired hand. But we all talked at great length and he proved himself to us."

Tom trained for the part of fighter pilot Pete "Maverick" Mitchell by spending three weeks with the pilots at Miramar, working out to add muscle, observing the real jet jockeys in action, and even riding in F-14s, which he called "just thrilling." When it was time to go before the cameras with costars Val Kilmer, Kelly McGillis, and Anthony Edwards, he delivered his usual intense performance. After filming was complete, he continued to be very involved with the development of the project—more involved than a 24-year-old actor who had appeared in fewer than 10 movies might otherwise expect to be. The producers allowed him to suggest how the final film should be edited. "In the rough cut the aerial story just didn't work," Cruise told the movie magazine *Premier*. "Tony Scott had miles and miles of aerial footage. He had to go back and tighten it up, define the story more. I always try to look at a rough cut like, 'The movie's not out yet—you can fix it.'"

In another interview he added, "Once a film comes out, they say, 'Oh, of course, that's why he took it. It's a commercial movie; a hit! Why wouldn't he want to do that?' People don't understand the risk factor. It didn't start out as a commercial movie. Nothing is a sure thing! Nothing is a sure thing! And if you looked at the script beforehand and saw what might have happened . . ."

When it was finished, *Top Gun* focused on competition between Maverick and a pilot nicknamed "Iceman" (Kilmer). Both want to be the best pilot at the Miramar training school. During training, Maverick becomes romantically involved with a civilian instructor played by McGillis. The movie also shows how Maverick deals

Tom gets advice from director Tony Scott while filming Top Gun. *Despite Cruise's youth and relative inexperience, he was allowed input into the script and the editing of the film. His changes and suggestions helped* Top Gun *earn $177 million.*

with the death of his best friend (Edwards) in an accident caused by Maverick's aggressive flying. At the end of the film, during an aerial duel between American and Soviet pilots, Maverick confronts his fears and his feelings about his friend's death to save Iceman—and the day for the United States.

Millions flocked to see Cruise and Kilmer compete in the skies and on the ground. Moviegoers were blown away by the thunderous excitement of the 50,000-pound jets, which roared across the screen in their feverish fight against the enemy. The awesome dance of each jet's crew-coordinated takeoff from the pitching deck of an aircraft carrier contrasted with the fierce crescendo of the planes' fiery thrusts as they ascended skyward. Audiences also enjoyed the romantic sparks that flew between Cruise and McGillis. As a result, *Top Gun* became the top-grossing movie of 1986, making more than $175 million. There was a fringe benefit for the U.S. Navy as well: the hoped-for increase in new recruits. "It's been a good thing all around," said Navy Secretary John F. Lehman Jr. "We're seeing real beneficial impacts in recruiting around the country. Recruiting centers are telling us that people are lining up to come in."

Aside from the enormous profit and the navy's delight in the new recruits, however, *Top Gun* generated a backlash of criticism over the film's celebration of aggressive, warlike behavior. Filmmaker Oliver Stone, a Vietnam veteran, was one of the most outspoken of the film's critics. In a December 1986 interview in *New York* magazine, he said, "You see a film like *Top Gun* if you're a kid, you join the navy. It looks great. I join the navy, I get to wear that spiffy uniform, I get to ride at the speed of light, I get the machine under my legs so I get that sexual energy, plus I get Kelly McGillis if I blow up the MIG! Nobody mentions the fact that he possibly started World War III by doing that! So the message of the movie is 'I get a girlfriend if I start World War III.'"

Despite this criticism, the huge success of *Top Gun* made one thing obvious: Tom Cruise was the hottest actor of his generation. His name was now equated with box-office drawing power, and his brilliant smile and penetrating eyes led to a label as a new American icon.

But before all the *Top Gun* hype, another American icon had sought Tom Cruise for a part in his next film. Blue-eyed Paul Newman, a charming, sexy actor who maintained the power to mesmerize audiences into his sixties, had signed on with director Martin Scorsese to make a sequel to Newman's 1961 classic *The Hustler*.

In that movie Newman played a young two-bit pool player named Eddie Felson, who challenges pool legend Minnesota Fats to a game. *The Hustler* is considered by many to have been Newman's best screen performance ever. The sequel, *The Color of Money*, is set 25 years after the original movie. Felson is no longer hustling; instead, he is teaching a young pool-playing protégé, hoping for a shot at winning big money. The role of the young Vincent Lauria was perfect for Tom Cruise, Newman felt, and he suggested that Scorsese contact the actor.

Cruise was thrilled to be considered for the role and was excited to work with both Newman and Scorsese, whose directing credits included such films as *Raging Bull*, *Mean Streets*, and *Taxi Driver*. To accurately portray a pool hustler, Tom haunted the smoke-filled pool halls of New York to sop up the flavor of life on the green felt. "It's not the money for these guys; it's the hustle," Tom found out. "One day they're up a hundred thousand dollars. The next day they'll go to the track and blow it all. They justify it, the morality."

A professional pool player was hired to freshen up Newman's already good game and to teach Tom, who did not know how to play. It wasn't easy for the young actor. "I worked day and night for months. For one shot, Marty told me, 'Okay now, the camera's just going to follow you around the table, and you got to clear off the whole table. You think you can do that, kid?' I go, 'yeah,' and I went home, and I was just sweating. So I really had to learn to play. But for me, that's exciting. The more I learned about playing pool, the more confident I became. I love pool now."

Cruise and Newman became close friends during the filming of *The Color of Money*, and the older actor was impressed by Tom's talent and work ethic. "He'll hang himself out to dry to seek something. He's not afraid

of looking like a ninny. He doesn't protect himself or his ego," Newman said. "And he's a wonderful experimenter. . . . He has what he needs to be a good actor." At the same time, the younger actor welcomed the opportunity to learn from both his veteran costar and the experienced director. In fact, *The Color of Money* was a perfect project for Tom, as everyone involved shared his desire to make the film as good as possible. Newman had insisted that the sequel be better than the original, and Scorsese is a demanding director who always strives for artistic excellence in his films. "We wanted this movie to stand on its own," said Scorsese. "The only link to *The Hustler* is the character of Fast Eddie. He's no longer a pool player. He's now on the

The Color of Money *starred veteran actor Paul Newman as Eddie Felson in a sequel to his 1961 hit* The Hustler; *Tom Cruise played his young protégé, Vincent Lauria. The two stars became good friends during filming. They were both praised for their performances, with Newman winning an Oscar for Best Actor.*

outside of the game looking in, and with a whole new perspective."

The pairing of Cruise and Newman—the old and the new American icons—drew great attention even before *The Color of Money* was released in 1987. The film did well at the box office, pulling in $6.4 million in its first week and a total of $52 million. Critically, both Newman and Cruise received high praise. *Newsweek*'s David Ansen wrote, "The casting of Newman and Cruise is more than just the casting coup of the year. Anyone who doubted Tom's seriousness as an actor will have to think again after seeing this whirlwind display." The *Village Voice* noted, "The film's revelation is Cruise— it's a loose, surprisingly vulnerable performance. Cruise is almost the best thing in the movie." The Hollywood establishment recognized Newman's performance with the Oscar for Best Actor, and the actor sent a telegram of thanks to Cruise, saying that the award belonged to both of them because Tom "did such a good job."

Because of the close friendship—almost a father-son relationship—that had developed between the two actors, it should be no surprise that Cruise asked Newman for advice when he considered marrying. The lady in question was actress Mimi Rogers, six years older than Cruise at age 31.

Like Cruise, Rogers had experienced divorce as a child. Mimi's mother had left home, and Mimi and her younger brother were left with their father, who, like Tom's father, was an engineer. Their family moved an inordinate number of times, and Mimi always felt like an outsider during her school years because of the constant change as well as the fact that her intelligence allowed her to skip several grades. She graduated from high school when she was 14 and spent five years volunteering in a hospital, counseling drug addicts and aiding

Millions of female fans' hopes were dashed when Cruise married actress Mimi Rogers in May of 1987. The bride, 31, and groom, 25, had a brief honeymoon in London following the wedding, before Cruise went back to work. Although Tom publicly expressed his happiness with the union, the marriage lasted less than three years.

Vietnam War veterans. She then went into acting, doing many television parts before landing some minor big-screen roles.

Mimi was taller than Tom, but he looked up to her for more reasons than that: "I like bright, sexy women. And strong, someone whom I'm not going to run over, someone strong enough to stand up to me. She's also got to have her own thing going. I don't want someone living for me."

Newman gave his blessing, and Tom and Mimi were married May 9, 1987, at a private ceremony to which only a few relatives and friends were invited. Actor Emilio Estevez, a friend from *The Outsiders*, was the best man. Tom and Mimi had a brief honeymoon/business trip in London before Cruise headed back onto the career track.

Tom's next role was not nearly as meaty as that of Vincent Lauria in *The Color of Money*. The film was a flashy no-brainer called *Cocktail*, in which Cruise played a Manhattan bartender who falls in love with a rich woman, played by Elisabeth Shue. Australian actor Bryan Brown played the young barman's mentor. Research for this light fare was fun for Tom, in that it entailed hanging around some of New York's more famous watering holes. At some of them he was even given the opportunity to mix drinks for thirsty customers.

Although the Cruise name helped *Cocktail* pull in more than $70 million, the reviews were scathing. Roger Ebert wrote, "This is the kind of movie that uses Tom's materialism as a target all through the story and then rewards him for it in the end. The more you think about what really happens in *Cocktail*, the more you realize how empty and fabricated it really is." *Video Movie Guide* gave *Cocktail* its "Turkey" rating and claimed Tom "substituted vacuous grins for acting."

That bit of fluff over with, Tom set about to film with

another Hollywood legend.

Dustin Hoffman's teenage daughter had a crush on Tom Cruise at the time he was being considered for the role of Charlie, the brother of Hoffman's character in *Rain Man*. The movie about two brothers, one autistic and the other a sleazy con man, seemed an improbable vehicle for the younger actor. Hoffman had originally been scheduled to play the con man, and Bill Murray was to take the autistic role. But Hoffman lobbied to play the autistic Raymond, a role he considered more challenging. Cruise was suggested for the con man role.

Rain Man went into development limbo for a while after Hoffman and Cruise were signed onto the lead roles. Once director Barry Levinson signed onto the project, *Rain Man* was a go.

Dustin Hoffman was originally cast to play the part of con man Charlie Babbitt in Rain Man, *but he convinced director Barry Levinson to cast him as the autistic Raymond instead. The role of Charlie, along with a $10 million paycheck, went to Cruise.*

Dustin Hoffman has been labeled a notorious perfectionist: obsessive, monomaniacal, and a major problem for directors, producers, and screenwriters alike. However, Hoffman and Cruise worked exceedingly well together, to the point of becoming friends as they filmed *Rain Man*.

"He's a demon," Dustin said of Tom in a later interview. "He gets up early, he works out, he goes home early, he studies, he works out again at night. He watches his diet as though he's an old fart like me. He doesn't drink. He doesn't smoke. He's very Spartan while making a film. And he always wanted to rehearse. It affected me emotionally, being in his presence."

Of Hoffman, Tom said, "Meeting him was intimidating. Sometimes I'd be watching the rushes and I'd just sit back and say, 'Wow! That's Dustin Hoffman.' But Dustin's not pretentious. He doesn't remind you he's a genius."

Tom took a risk in playing Charlie. Charlie is materialistic and callow. He doesn't even know he has an autistic brother until he finds out his father has willed $3 million to an unknown sibling, Raymond. Subsequently Charlie kidnaps Raymond in an attempt to get the inheritance. Some viewers were upset because the film does not have a happy ending. Although at the movie's end it is apparent Charlie has grown emotionally attached to his disabled brother, it was hard to read those feelings on Tom's face, because he had inexplicably donned a pair of dark sunglasses.

As for Hoffman, he had studied the subject of autism intensely in order to play Raymond more realistically. Throughout the film, he never made eye contact with Charlie, and he affected a particular walk and a head tic.

Although in 1988 Tom Cruise was rated the number one box office star for the second time since 1986, Dustin Hoffman won the Oscar for Best Actor for his role as Raymond in *Rain Man*. The picture also received the Oscar for Best Picture, and Barry Levinson received an Oscar for Best Director. While Cruise was left out in the rain with no nominations or awards, in the end, he added more than $10 million to his bank account.

"People asked after *Rain Man*," Cruise said, "'How are you going to match the success of that picture?' I said, 'I can't live my life by what is going to make $20 or $100 million.' I don't know what is going to happen to my career. I am going to take a lot of risks and some of it is going to work and some of it is not going to work. Some of it will be trash and some of it, I hope, will be good. I make the decisions. I pick the scripts. I have only myself to blame if things don't work out. That is the way I want to live my life. That is the way I set out to live it at the beginning."

Cruise placed his handsome, All-American boy image at risk by playing the role of paralyzed Vietnam veteran Ron Kovic (pictured in the center, with director Oliver Stone at right) in Born on the Fourth of July. *The payoff was a Golden Globe Award for Best Actor and his first Academy Award nomination.*

6

RIDING THE CREST

MOVIE DIRECTOR OLIVER STONE is a decorated veteran of the Vietnam war, and his 1986 picture *Platoon* was called "the best film made on the subject of Vietnam" and won an Oscar for Best Picture. In 1989 he responded cinematically to the movie he had hated three years earlier, *Top Gun*. In his film *Born on the Fourth of July*, he cast *Top Gun's* hotshot fighter pilot, Tom Cruise, as an impotent cripple, permanently scarred both physically and emotionally by the Vietnam War.

The film was based on the book of the same name written by former U.S. Marine Ron Kovic, who had been shot and paralyzed while serving in Vietnam. Feeling neglected and betrayed by the country he had sworn to serve and protect, Kovic wrote a scathing indictment of war and the horrors of its aftermath as he experienced them in his life after returning from Vietnam. When Stone read Kovic's book in the late 1970s, he sought out the fellow veteran. Subsequently, the two worked on a screen adaptation of the book, and Al Pacino was chosen to play Kovic in the movie. Just as production was to get under way,

however, the Pacino deal fell through and the project came
to a halt. Kovic was devastated, but Stone remained committed to someday bringing Kovic's dream of making the
film to fruition.

By 1988 Stone had directed such brilliant films as
Platoon, *Salvador*, and *Wall Street*. He discussed the idea
of a film about the horrible aftereffects of the Vietnam War
with Cruise, and then took the actor to meet Kovic. Tom
immediately bonded with the wheelchair-bound ex-soldier.
At the time, Stone had little money for the project, but Tom
did not want to pass up the chance to work with the red-hot
director, so he deferred his usual acting fees until the production went into the black.

Tom Cruise was taking an enormous risk in accepting a
role that could conceivably blow his pretty, all-American-
boy image out the window. Even the film studio balked at
distributing promotional photos showing Tom in a wheel-
chair. For the first time on screen, Tom would be seen in
the most degrading personal situations, particularly in the
hospital segments, which depicted the squalor and filth that
severely disabled soldiers had to helplessly endure when
they returned stateside.

In the process of immersing himself in the very different world paraplegics inhabit, Tom discovered that he and
Ron Kovic had a few things in common. Both were raised
in the Catholic religion, and both came from families that
had suffered hard times. Ron came to trust completely in
Tom's ability to act out his story faithfully.

A former marine captain was enlisted to train Tom and
other actors in the rudiments of soldiering. Battle scenes
were filmed in the jungles of the Philippines. Tom lost
weight to achieve a gaunt and shriveled look for the film's
later scenes when Ron became wheelchair-bound after
months of poor treatment in the hospital.

Cruise received much critical acclaim for his efforts,
and for the first time in his career he was nominated for an
Oscar for Best Actor. Although Cruise did not win, Oliver

Stone won an Oscar for Best Director and in his acceptance speech praised Tom Cruise for "making Ron's dream come true." Cruise did win a Golden Globe Award for his portrayal of the young Kovic, and the crippled veteran himself was so pleased with Tom's performance that he gave the actor the Bronze Star that he had kept in a box by his bed for 21 years. "I told him it was for his heroic performance," Ron said.

At the time *Born on the Fourth of July* was being filmed, Tom Cruise and Mimi Rogers were in their third year of marriage. But the month the movie was released, December 1989, the couple separated. By the time the Oscars rolled around in early spring, Tom had divorced Mimi. Characteristically, Tom has never divulged the real reason behind the Cruise-Rogers split. In January 1990, the month he filed for divorce, Tom had told a *Rolling Stone* interviewer "I couldn't imagine being without her or being alone. I care about my wife more than anything in the world. She's my best friend. I love her." Shortly after that, however, Tom released a statement that said, "While there have been positive aspects to our marriage, there were some issues that couldn't be resolved, even after working on them for a period of time."

In the wake of his marriage's failure and *Born on the Fourth of July*'s success, Cruise needed to start thinking about his next career move. He decided to combine his career with a hobby that he had become passionate about, auto racing.

During the making of *The Color of Money,* Paul Newman had introduced Tom Cruise to one of his enduring passions: race car driving. After an early taste of the power and speed of auto racing, Cruise enrolled in the Bob Bondurant School of High Performance Driving to learn as much as he could about the sport. He also paid for *Top Gun* producer Don Simpson to attend the school with him. Simpson finished the driving course at the top of the class, with Tom a respectable third. "I have been in a car with

Tom in Rome, in San Francisco, in Los Angeles, and each time he was in the driver's seat and I was truly scared," the producer later said. "This is a man who is comfortable taking major risks. He likes to be out there on the edge, whether it's in the car or on the screen."

"I think one of the great things in life is the feeling of accomplishment, choosing a goal and achieving it," Tom said of his hobby. "I get that sensation with racing. I love the intensity of it and the demands, physically and emotionally."

Having gotten his feet wet on the racing circuit, Cruise decided that he wanted to make a movie about auto racing. He felt he understood the dynamics involved, because he believed making movies is like racing cars. In both endeavors, total dedication, which translates into long work days, is required. Also, a family-like commitment evolves among racing team members that is similar to the camaraderie generated on a movie set.

Tom got together with Simpson and Jerry Bruckheimer, and the three began breathing some life into the project. With writer Bob Towne, Tom roughed out a script about drivers and speed, culminating in the Daytona 500. *Top Gun* director Tony Scott was hired to shoot the film, and respected actor Robert Duvall signed on to play the father figure to Tom. Australian actress Nicole Kidman was selected to play the female lead.

Cruise had first noticed Kidman when he watched her on-screen in *Dead Calm*, a stylish thriller in which Nicole and costar Sam Neill are terrorized at sea by a maniac. Tom was immediately taken. Taller than Tom by inches, with wild red hair and a willowy figure, Nicole was an independent woman who was very serious about her acting career. As sparks flew on-screen, the two began to see each other regularly outside of work as well.

Days of Thunder was released over the Fourth of July weekend, 1990. Although the film received mixed reviews, it grossed a respectable $80 million at the box office. Tom had a great time racing, suffering just a few bumps and bruises in the process. The scripted sizzle between Tom and love interest Nicole on the set was actually enhanced by the obvious real-life chemistry between the two.

Nearly six months after the release of *Days of Thunder*, on Christmas Eve 1990, Tom and Nicole went before a civil judge and were married in the company of a select number of friends and relatives. In an interview five years later, Cruise remarked, "I say to myself, thank God I made the right choice in marrying her, and was fortunate enough that she said yes. I knew she was it for me. I absolutely knew—I just knew it. I just knew I couldn't live without her. It's the best decision I ever made."

Although life seemed perfect for the newlyweds, they couldn't translate their offscreen magic into on-screen success in their next movie together, 1991's ambitious *Far and Away*. For this film, Tom returned to the Mapother homeland, Ireland, to shoot the epic story of a poor Irish laborer trying to survive in the late 19th century. Joseph, played by Tom, becomes obsessed with killing the landowner who torches his father's house because his father can no longer afford to rent the property. Instead of murdering the man, Joseph himself is beaten within an inch of his life by the cruel landowner, who then allows the young man to recuperate from his wounds within his spacious mansion.

Enter Nicole Kidman as the landowner's daughter, Shannon. Her fiery temperament has made her a rebel in her own family, and Joseph becomes enamored with her during his stay. They meet again later by chance, and since Joseph's fortunes have not increased a jot toward prosperity and Shannon's rebelliousness has turned to wanderlust, the two decide to make for America. They travel as brother and sister and debark in Boston. Joseph becomes a boxer for hire, fighting any comers, and Shannon plucks feathers from chickens. His romantic interest in Shannon is as antagonistic as the rest of his

As his marriage to Mimi Rogers was ending, Cruise found happiness in love with Australian actress Nicole Kidman. The two met while filming the race car drama Days of Thunder, *and their chemistry was evident in the film's love scenes. The film premiered in July of 1990 and the two were wed less than six months later.*

character. Instead of recognizing their inevitable romantic connection, they verbally spar throughout most of the movie. The two do agree to save enough money to flee to the great American West and take part in the Oklahoma land rush, staking out a claim on a small plot of land.

Tom had to learn how to ride a horse and speak in an Irish brogue for the film. Critics felt he pulled off the former better than the latter. Studio publicity releases for *Far and Away* did not mention that Tom and Nicole were married, and a *New York City Daily News* review claimed the movie had "surprisingly little passion or electricity in this boisterous period love story." A *New York Times* critic complained, "This film is as much an epic event as sitting at home watching television." Film critic Roger Ebert wasn't impressed with Ron Howard's efforts either: "It's depressing that such a lavish and expensive production, starring an important actor like Tom Cruise, could be devoted to such a shallow story. Do they think audiences have entirely lost their wits?" he asked. Ebert claimed the story line was a hodgepodge of "old boxing movies," and added, "Shannon and Joseph are equally characters, completely victims of the story, denied all personality attributes except those routinely assigned to captives of genre fiction. Do they realize they have nothing intelligent, witty, or unexpected to say in the entire movie?"

Director Ron Howard evidently saw more romantic electricity between the newlyweds than the critics believed came through on the screen. Howard said that while Tom and Nicole were on the set, they acted like a pair of honeymooners, oohing and aahing at each other whenever they could.

But in the end, *Far and Away* had to be considered a major disappointment. It did not even make projected box office figures. But even though Cruise was criticized for his $12 million paycheck, one Hollywood producer

Tom led an all-star cast that included Jack Nicholson, Kevin Bacon, and Demi Moore in 1992's A Few Good Men. *While he had trouble tackling some of his character's complicated legal jargon because of his dyslexia, he managed to convincingly play a driven lawyer trying to get at the truth behind the murder of a young Marine.*

insisted that "Tom Cruise didn't bomb. The movie bombed."

In his next film Tom was surrounded by a superstar cast that included Jack Nicholson, Kevin Bacon, Kiefer Sutherland, Demi Moore, and Kevin Pollak. *A Few Good Men* was a tense drama centered on the trial of two marines accused of murder. Tom once again drew from his real-life past for the role, in which his character is forced to deal with the legacy of his father. His Mapother family tradition also came into play, as his character was a lawyer. Tom garnered the highest salary of all the cast members: a whopping $12.5 million.

Tom was cast in the familiar role of a problem kid forced to turn hero. But the verbal requirements of the role of lawyer Lieutenant Daniel Kaffee were tougher than any he had faced in his previous films, particularly considering his trials with dyslexia. Costar Kevin Bacon also had problems mastering the legal terms, so the two actors teamed up for rehearsals. "It was completely foreign to me, and, to a certain extent, to him," Bacon said. "It was exhausting but fun. That's why you act." Director Rob Reiner concurred with Bacon's assessment of the difficult dialogue: "[Tom] went to work, studied the terminology. He really steeped himself in it."

Tom pulled off the legalese in the courtroom against powerhouse Nicholson with an ease that did not make him look like he was playing second fiddle to the veteran actor. Tom was said to have been friendly to Nicholson on the set, but not as star-struck as he had been working with Paul Newman and Dustin Hoffman. Perhaps this was because Tom was now 30 years old and a hugely successful actor in his own right. Cruise teased Nicholson by doing an imitation of him, much to the enjoyment of the cast; the imitation was even incorporated into the movie.

When *A Few Good Men* was released in December 1992, it went up against several other blockbusters, including *The Bodyguard*, *Dracula*, and *Aladdin*. Nevertheless, the movie did very well at the box office, earning more than $100 million, and garnered four Academy Award nominations, including Best Picture. Cruise was not nominated for an Oscar, although costar Jack Nicholson was, but he did receive a Golden Globe nomination for his performance.

In 1993, Tom starred in the hit film The Firm, *made his directorial debut with the Showtime film* The Frightening Frammies, *and adopted a baby girl, Isabella Jane Kidman Cruise. That same year, he had his handprints immortalized in cement outside Mann's Chinese Theater in Hollywood.*

7

STAYING ABOVE
THE CLOUDS

TOM CRUISE ONCE said, "I'd love to have kids. I'd turn down an Oscar to see my little boy in a baseball game or my little girl in a song and dance recital." That dream came true for him in 1993, when he and Kidman adopted a baby girl, Isabella Jane Kidman Cruise.

Tom spoke of his new infant daughter at the Golden Globe awards ceremony a scant week after her adoption. "Becoming a father is the greatest thing that has ever happened to me," he said. "I have longed for a child for so long. Now that I have little Isabella, I look at her and thank God every day for giving me such a precious gift. I adore her to death and I hope I will love and protect her to my dying day—I am ecstatically happy. Isabella comes before everything—career, films, business, everything. The baby and Nicole are the most important things in my life. Becoming a father makes you realize what it is all about."

Parenting seemed to come naturally to Tom and Nicole, and as "Bella" grew from infancy, she was seen more often with either or both of the actors in public.

Also in 1993, Tom Cruise spawned another block-buster movie with the release of *The Firm,* which again positioned him near the top of the box office draws for that year. A spate of lawyer novels had captured the reading public's imagination and dollars, and they flocked to see the ever-popular actor flesh out author John Grisham's hero on the screen. Tom was paid a handsome $15 million for the role, in which he is torn between his moral beliefs and the lure of the lucrative lifestyle offered by his company, which is involved in illegal activities.

The Firm was directed by noted filmmaker Sydney Pollack, who was later criticized for the film's length, two-and-a-half hours. The movie is suspenseful with less action and violence than big pictures typically feature. Tom's character, Mitch Deere, is a young lawyer hired for a lot of money by a prestigious law firm in Memphis. Excited by the prospect of status and wealth, the hard-working and idealistic Mitch is chagrined to discover his new employer's ties to the underworld. He makes off with incriminating evidence and is pursued by his firm, the Mob, and the FBI.

Novelist John Grisham was pleased that Cruise was hired for the role of Mitch. Director Pollack had nothing but praise for Tom, calling him "the most voraciously curious actor I have ever worked with. He's dying to learn. . . . He has much more range than many people realize. He throws himself into his roles with no vanity at all. . . . I expect great things from him."

The film, which also featured Gene Hackman, Holly Hunter, and Ed Harris, knocked *Jurassic Park* out of its top position upon its summer 1993 release. It surpassed $100 million within 23 days, a return only a handful of other movies have bested.

Tom broke some new professional ground in 1993 with his directorial debut for a Showtime cable television effort called *The Frightening Frammies.* Since first making a serious name for himself with *Risky Business* in the 1980s, Tom had been allowed an increasing amount of influence on his subsequent film productions. He had wanted to give directing a try, and fared rather well critically with this story penned by crime writer Jim Thompson.

Tom received $70,000 for the production, which obviously was not a large amount for an actor who receives more than 200 times that amount per picture, but he found directing quite a challenging experience. For a person who usually works in multimillion-dollar productions, he found that the show's $700,000 budget required some strategic thinking on his part.

Tom Cruise's most startling transformation yet, however, was a physical one that occurred in 1994 when he was cast as the vampire Lestat in the movie *Interview with the Vampire*. Long golden hair framed Tom's gaunt, pale face as his blood-drenched mouth grinned, grimaced, and groaned through his role as mentor to his angst-filled protégé, Louis, played by Brad Pitt.

The movie was based on a novel by Ann Rice, who initially vehemently protested the casting of Tom Cruise as her anti-hero, Lestat. She and her fans even took to bad-mouthing him in public, which generated a lot of anticipation for the movie and for Tom Cruise's performance in particular. Rice's denunciations bothered Tom but nevertheless increased his resolve to play the part. Tom lost 18 pounds for the role, read all of Rice's works (despite his dyslexia), took piano lessons, toured the museums of Paris, practiced speaking with European diction, and studied films of animal killings. He also bleached his hair, eyebrows, and body hair for the part.

Upon seeing a prerelease copy of the film, Rice completely changed her mind; she adored Tom's performance and even hinted at a sequel. Cruise appeared on-screen as though he enjoyed enacting the story of the young Louis's induction into the netherworld of vampires. The story unfolds in the present with the 200-year-old Louis being interviewed by journalist Daniel Malloy, played by Christian Slater (a replacement for River Phoenix, who had just died of a drug overdose). Louis, a reluctant vampire, relates the burden of Lestat's influence over him these many years, and reveals that he has attempted several times to kill the evil Lestat (which he felt really guilty about).

Tom's portrayal of Lestat showed an actor more and more willing to step beyond his previous roles, many of which portrayed a young guy with a moral dilemma who just happens to have a cute young woman nearby to loyally encourage him onto the right path. This was the first time that Tom had played the villain's role.

Christian Slater commented later about the some of Tom's methodology during the filming of *Interview*. "Before the cameras would start rolling, Tom would be getting into it," Slater said, "and he'd say things to me like, 'I'm going to rip your throat out, you filthy. . .' He was helpful that way."

Anne Rice's novels have quite a following; fans of her books, together with the millions who habitually flock to Tom Cruise films, combined to make this effort a financial success. The movie made more than $100 million in the United States. As a *New York Times* reviewer put it, "Cruise is flabbergastingly right for this role. The vampire Lestat brings out in Cruise a fiery, mature sexual magnetism he has not previously displayed on the screen."

When his next film was released, Tom was back to looking like his regular Hollywood idol self. Baby boomers weren't the only ones excited by all the pre-publicity hype for *Mission: Impossible,* which was freely based on the hit 1960s television series of the same

Long, golden hair, a pale face, and blood-drenched fangs caused many Cruise fans to do a double-take when he portrayed the vampire Lestat in the film adaptation of Ann Rice's novel Interview with the Vampire. *It marked the first time that Tom played an outright villain on-screen. The film did well, grossing more than $100 million in the United States.*

name. The idea for the movie had been floating around Hollywood for about 10 years, and the series had been a particular favorite of Tom's when he was a youngster. He jumped at the chance to star in it and use it as the first project in his fledgling production company. Tom partnered this company—called Odin, after the king of the Viking gods—with his long-time publicity agent and friend, Paula Wagner. Tom deferred a salary for this first production from Odin Studios and settled on a percentage of the profits instead. Tom was adamant about not exceeding the film's budget or its schedule, a position that sometimes put him at odds with director Brian De Palma.

Action movies had proven to be the surefire hits of the 1990s, and *Mission: Impossible*, about a top secret government espionage unit, promised to be an action mega-blockbuster. Tom was excited about his starring role in the part made famous by Peter Graves. The movie was shot on location in Prague, and in Pinewood Studios in London, where Tom had shot *Interview with the Vampire*.

As the movie played out, Tom was involved in three extravagantly dangerous scenes. The most dangerous required him to catapult himself through the glass of a huge aquarium, followed by a 30-foot wave of water. Director De Palma insisted that Tom do the scene himself to make the shot convincing. "And he did it," De Palma said later. "But I swear he could have drowned."

Screenwriter David Koepp reiterated the traits Tom Cruise's peers have praised him for throughout his film career: "He's incredibly persistent and focused, and he'll drive you completely insane because he keeps coming at it and at it and at it. But then you realize that because he's gone at it, you're going to go at it."

Tom experienced an extra benefit during filming by

having his daughter, Isabella, and his new young son, Connor Antony Kidman Cruise, on the set each day. Nicole and Tom had adopted Connor, an African-American child, in 1995. The children had an American nanny, but the doting parents spent as much time as possible doing family activities like going to the park. Tom even brought Connor to a planning meeting with De Palma and the other actors. Tom silenced the meeting when Connor, who had had a sleepless night, dozed off.

Mission: Impossible received mixed reviews from the press and the public upon its release. Whereas all agreed the action scenes were spectacular, many found the plot too difficult to follow. The movie nevertheless made a fortune—more than $400 million.

Back in Los Angeles, one thing Tom had not planned on was unscripted heroics. While driving down the street, he witnessed an accident: a woman was hit by a car. Tom immediately stopped his car at an angle to protect her injured body, phoned for help, then waited as emergency personnel attended to her. He followed the ambulance to the UCLA Medical Center. The woman, Heloise Vinhas, who was an aspiring actress, suffered a broken leg and bruised ribs. Upon learning that she had no medical insurance, Tom covered her $7,000 bill. Only later did Vinhas realize who her good Samaritan was. "Tom is a very nice man, the best," she said.

Tom Cruise's winning streak continued with the 1997 release of *Jerry Maguire*, directed by Cameron Crowe. Tom played an aggressive sports agent who finds himself out of the high-stakes game when he decides he doesn't care for some of the "rules." Tom's character, Jerry, is generally likable in his anxiety to make a name for himself in the midst of trying to discover just who he really is (which isn't necessarily always a nice guy). Not

As down-and-out sports agent Jerry Maguire, Cruise relied on his only remaining client, Rod Tidwell (played by Cuba Gooding Jr.), a talented but temperamental football player. The film was released during the Christmas season of 1997 and earned Cruise a second Academy Award nomination.

surprisingly, a lovely young single mother, played by Renée Zellweger, and her darling young son gently ease Jerry through his dilemma and onto the right path by the movie's end.

The movie received very good reviews from most critics, and Cruise was nominated for a Best Actor Oscar. Once again, however, he was passed over for an Academy Award, although costar Cuba Gooding Jr. won an Oscar for Best Supporting Actor for his enthusiastic portrayal of an egocentric football player.

L. Ron Hubbard (1911–1986), a science-fiction writer, gained fame and notoriety by founding the Church of Scientology. His "religion" has been the focus of negative attention and media scrutiny since the 1950s.

8

MYTH, MEANING, AND MYSTERY

A CHURCH AFFILIATION seems to border on the mysterious or weird when, even though the member exhibits no untoward external behavior, the organization to which he belongs is constantly the focus of negative attention. Such has been the case with Tom Cruise and the Church of Scientology.

By 1989 Tom had completed his first basic courses in Scientology. He was married to Mimi Rogers at the time, and she had been involved in the church since she was a teenager. Nicole Kidman came to the church after she married Tom in 1990. Tom is known as a good friend of the present head of the Church of Scientology, David Miscavige. Shortly after Tom's marriage to Nicole, a dinner was held in their honor; Miscavige was seated next to Tom, and two tables full of Scientologists were placed nearby.

What is now called the Church of Scientology was founded in the 1950s by L. Ron Hubbard, known at that time as a prolific science fiction writer. In 1950 he wrote the first of many of Scientology's sacred texts, called *Dianetics: The Modern Science of Mental*

Health. In it he introduced the practice of *auditing*.

Hubbard claimed auditing was necessary to cure human beings of the residual effects of events that occurred 75 million years ago. According to Hubbard, 70 planets formed a galactic federation at that time. Taxation, repressive governmental tactics, and overpopulation combined to make life a far cry from nirvana.

Scientology presently publishes and distributes a hefty tome that fully outlines its teachings and practices. In it, the process of auditing promises "a person can rid himself of his reactive mind and the limitations it imposes upon him—limitations which were once thought 'natural.'" Scientology calls the disabling thoughts and patterns in a person's reactive mind *engrams*. The purpose of auditing is to erase the engrams, thereby nullifying their harmful energy. The tool Hubbard designed to assist in the auditing process is called an *E-meter*, a device rather like a lie detector that registers electrical changes in the skin as a person reveals his or her most intimate thoughts to the auditor.

Hubbard said his varied auditing processes would take a person down a guaranteed path to success. Through auditing, Hubbard claimed, an individual would "achieve greater awareness, higher states of existence and ultimately, a recognition of his own immortal nature."

Lafayette Ronald Hubbard was born in Nebraska in 1911. He served in World War II and contacted the Veterans Administration in 1947 complaining about suicidal impulses and a mind seriously affected by the trauma of war. Psychological troubles notwithstanding, he began to make a successful living as a science fiction writer. Speaking before a writers' convention in 1949, Hubbard stated that if a person really wanted to make a million dollars, the best way would be to start his own religion. Within a year he had published *Dianetics: The Modern Science of Mental Health*, which was an immediate and continuing financial success.

Years after the church had gotten into full swing, its literature began to publish Hubbard's war service as that of an extensively decorated hero who had been crippled and blinded during combat. Hubbard claimed he was twice pronounced dead and had his life and sight restored through the power of Scientology.

Interestingly enough, and much to the dismay of the Dyslexia Foundation of America, in 1992 Tom Cruise stated that Scientology had cured his dyslexia. Tom said, "I was diagnosed as dyslexic a long time ago, took remedial courses all through school. Then I was given *The Basic Study Manual*, written by L. Ron Hubbard. I started applying its principles, began reading faster, and that convinced me I had never been dyslexic." The executive vice president of the Dyslexia Foundation at that time, Joyce Bulifant, was concerned that Tom's contention would make people think dyslexia could be cured as easily as any common everyday malady.

From its beginnings, L. Ron Hubbard's creation has had its detractors. Hubbard's self-proclaimed biographical information was attacked as well. He had accorded himself the honor of having a doctorate from Sequoia University. It was actually a fake mail order degree. During Hubbard's second divorce, which occurred in 1951, his wife accused him of being "hopelessly insane" and that he had "tortured her." In 1984, the church brought suit against a researcher working on Hubbard's biography. The conclusion reached by the California judge assigned the case was that Hubbard was a "pathological liar."

From the mid-1950s through the 1960s, however, Hubbard's enterprise had convinced so many people that Scientology could cure them of their disabling emotional baggage that the church had amassed $400 million. He added enough religious and spiritual convictions to his package of scientific freedom from man's ills that his organization was able to be called a "church," and it enjoyed tax-exempt status until 1967. At this time, Hubbard set sail on a 342-foot vessel named *Apollo*. He sailed for a while in international waters, safe from the hounding of government prosecutors, who were later able to prove he had been laundering millions of dollars collected from his followers through various phony schemes and secret Swiss bank accounts.

In 1991, a group called the Cult Awareness Network, organized to monitor hundreds of "mind control" cults throughout the country, described Scientology this way: "Scientology is quite likely the most ruthless, the most classically terroristic, the most litigious and the most lucrative cult the country has ever seen." Executive Director Cynthia Kisser added, "No cult extracts more money from its members."

In the 1980s, an hour's counseling session would cost between $200 and $1,000. If they didn't have the money, new recruits, which Scientology officials called "raw meat," would earn their session money by enlisting more recruits from the streets or by signing a billion-year work contract (which naturally included reincarnation) that allowed them to live on church premises with a $25 weekly allowance. These enlistees worked as many as 15 hours a day at menial jobs.

But celebrity members, such as Tom Cruise, John Travolta, Kirstie Alley, Anne Archer, and the late Sonny Bono to name a few, are treated to luxurious appointments housed in Celebrity Centers. These centers house study areas for Scientology courses as well as provide workshops focused on getting ahead in the television, movie, and music industries. Seminars include "How to

Make It as a TV Writer," "Artists Revitalization Work-shop," and "Success in the Music Industry."

Before Hubbard died in 1986, the person who probably knew more about Scientology than anyone else was a man named Ronald DeWolf. DeWolf was born Lafayette Ronald Hubbard Jr., but eventually changed his name and turned his life away from his father's pursuits. DeWolf referred to the church's followers as victims. "They are neurotic," he said in 1982. "They are people who are lost and adrift, spiritually and psychologically. They are people who have fears."

As a young uneducated adult, DeWolf was in charge

Mimi Rogers first introduced Cruise to Scientology after they were married. By 1989, Tom had completed his first basic courses in the church.

of training for the church and he was being groomed as the heir apparent. His father's credo, DeWolf said, was "to promise people anything but get their money."

Tom Cruise's penchant for revealing so little about his personal life may well have its roots in a "Code of Honor" Hubbard wrote for Scientologists sometime before his death. In part, the code states, "Do not give or receive communication unless you yourself desire it."

Although the organization is viewed as a legitimate religion in 62 countries, the German government vigorously opposes it as a threat to democracy, and Tom Cruise's movie *Mission: Impossible* was boycotted in Germany because of the actor's ties to the church. Fellow actor John Travolta, an outspoken Scientologist, has defended the church before a U.S.-based human rights panel in response to Germany's vehement opposition of the church.

Of Scientology Tom has said:

It's a very personal thing. Truly this is how I feel about it. People come up to me and ask me, "So what is Scientology?" I say, "Hey, if you want to know about it, then read a book about it and see what it means to you." It has certainly helped me. Very much so. It has helped my spiritual life. I enjoy it. But people try to create this whole thing about how Scientology is controlling my money and my career.

I can't tell anyone what their path to enlightenment is. It's their own adventure. But for me, Scientology is about self-discovery and deciding on my own what is real and true. I know people say that as a religion it dictates. But for me it's the reverse of that. I don't think it dictates anything. I believe it's directed towards conceptual thinking and independent ideas.

Perhaps the most positive endorsement of Scientology came in an off-the-cuff remark made by director Rob Reiner during a magazine interview. Reiner worked with Cruise on *A Few Good Men*. "Look, I don't know anything about Scientology, but if Scientology means you're the way Tom Cruise is, then everyone should be a Scientologist," said Reiner. "He cares, and he works his butt off."

Tom and Nicole worked and lived in London for 15 months in 1997 and 1998 while shooting director Stanley Kubrick's highly anticipated Eyes Wide Shut. *The film marks their first on-screen pairing since 1991's* Far and Away.

9

WHAT THE FUTURE HOLDS

SO WHAT WILL the millennium hold for this hot property christened Thomas Cruise Mapother IV? Can he do anything wrong? Anything that would dim the amazing brilliance of his career?

He and his wife, Nicole, whom he affectionately calls Nic, lived in London for 15 months with their children while working on the film *Eyes Wide Shut*. Stanley Kubrick—the director of such masterpieces as *A Clockwork Orange, Dr. Strangelove,* and *2001: A Space Odyssey*—is in charge of what has now become one of the longest film shoots in history. A tentative release date for the film is March 1999.

The film is another departure from Tom's normal good-guy image. The story centers on a pair of married psychiatrists (Tom and Nicole) who fantasize about other partners and betray each other. However, little is known about the plot, which has led to a lot of speculation in film industry magazines. "I've read a lot of stuff," Cruise told *A&E Biography Magazine* in October 1998. "No one has gotten it right. They're reaching."

Tom and Nicole have spent enough time over the years in England—and particularly in 1998 while filming *Eyes Wide Shut*—that they were reportedly house hunting, seeking something in the $3 million range. They also enrolled Isabella and Connor in a London preschool, although the family returned to the United States in the fall of 1998.

What next? Tom is expected to continue his production company, which has an exclusive deal with Paramount for multiple projects. Tom's office, once a suite used by the multimillionaire Howard Hughes, contains all the trappings of a Hollywood mogul's lair. And Tom Cruise has never tried to hide his ambition to direct. With each picture he has made, Tom has increased his involvement in the moviemaking process: script approval, casting approval, advertising approval, etc.

For the near future, Cruise and director Rob Reiner are planning to do a terrorist action film together. Also in negotiations is a possible role for Tom as Harry Houdini. Tom is director Paul Verhoeven's (*Total Recall, Starship Troopers*) top choice for the story of the famous magician's search for spiritual meaning after he narrowly survives death during a trick that goes wrong. Tom is also committed to a sequel to his hit *Mission: Impossible*.

Tom handles his fame well, enjoying his perks but also trying to lead a normal family life. "I don't like to put myself into situations where I get stared at a lot. On a screen, it's fine—in front of a crowd, I'll pass," he notes. Since adopting his two children, Tom has outfitted his Los Angeles mansion with security walls and a high-tech alarm system. He avoids traveling with an entourage of bodyguards, however, and instead enjoys skating with his family in New York's Central Park or taking Nicole to a movie. He is said to be somewhat

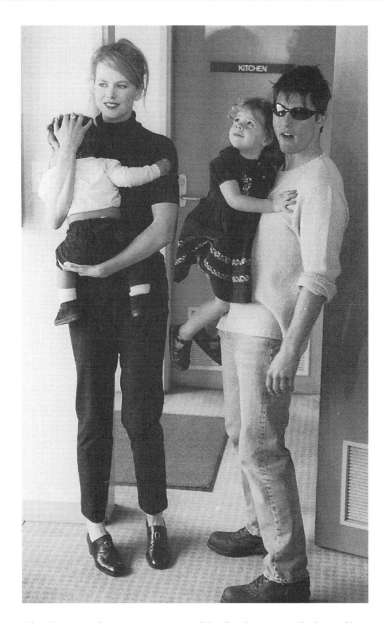

The Cruise-Kidman union is one of the few long-term, high-profile marriages to survive in Hollywood. Much of the couple's happiness together is in raising their two adopted children. "Becoming a father is the greatest thing that has ever happened to me," Tom said in 1993. "Becoming a father makes you realize what it is all about."

congenial in public, agreeing to sign autographs if approached politely. "I just treat people the way I want to be treated," he says.

"With Tom and Nic, you never feel like you're hanging out with movie stars—until you find yourself being chased down the street by 400 paparazzi," Australian actress Naomi Watts, a close friend of Kidman's, told *Vogue* in October 1995. "That's the only time you see them click out of being free spirits and think, 'OK, now I've got to keep my guard up.'"

Although he tries to guard his privacy, Tom understands that intense attention is one of the prices of great fame. In an interview about his stardom, he commented:

> I wake up every day and know I'm a lucky guy. . . . [T]his is where I want to be. You see some people who destroy themselves because they become successful and feel guilty about acknowledging it—and then it goes away. However terrible it is, I'm enjoying myself.

To Tom Cruise, making good movies is more important than making a lot of money, although he has been fortunate enough to do both. "You know, [making a lot of money is] a very small idea. That's too narrow a stake. The bigger one is: What can I do for myself, what can I do for the world, what can I do to make myself better, what-do-I-want-to-do? That's what's important."

Whatever force is guiding Tom Cruise's life shows no signs of leaving him behind on this skyrocketing ride to higher and higher heights. As a star who has overcome much adversity and as the recipient of some of the highest salaries in film history, Tom Cruise—only in his thirties—certainly lacks for nothing. But with him, it has never been simply a question of "showing him the money."

Of the time as a teenager when he first discovered his avocation, he has said, "I wanted to be an actor. I want it, wanted it very badly. I was hungry." On every film set Tom Cruise continues to prove by his work ethic that he is "still hungry."

CHRONOLOGY

1962 Thomas Cruise Mapother IV is born July 3 in Syracuse, New York

1974 Tom Mapother leaves his wife and children.

1978 Mary Lee Mapother marries Jack South; family moves to Glen Ridge, New Jersey

1980 Tom Cruise Mapother stars in Glen Ridge High School production of *Guys and Dolls*; decides to move to New York City after graduation and become an actor

1981 Changes name to Tom Cruise; has small part in film *Endless Love*, starring Brooke Shields and Martin Hewitt

1982 Selected for minor role in *Taps*, but given more important role of David Shawn after intense performance; Makes *Losin' It* with Shelley Long; joins a cast of young and talented actors (nicknamed the "Brat Pack") in *The Outsiders,* directed by Francis Ford Coppola

1983 Has first starring role, opposite Rebecca De Mornay, in *Risky Business*; begins dating De Mornay; *Risky Business* becomes a big hit, earning $63 million; makes *All the Right Moves*

1984 Visits with father just before his death from cancer

1985 Has a terrible time making the fantasy film *Legend* with Ridley Scott in London; reads script for movie about U.S. Navy pilots called *Top Gun*

1986 *Top Gun* makes $177 million and establishes Tom Cruise as the biggest box-office draw of his generation

1987 Makes *The Color of Money* with Paul Newman; marries Mimi Rogers, who introduces him to the Church of Scientology

1988 *Cocktail* is released, earning $78 million; Cruise's fee rises to $5 million per movie; makes *Rain Man* with Dustin Hoffman; meets crippled Vietnam veteran Ron Kovic

1989 Stars in *Born on the Fourth of July*

1990 Makes *Days of Thunder* with Nicole Kidman and Robert Duvall; divorces Mimi Rogers; marries Kidman

1991 Epic *Far and Away*, also starring Kidman, does poorly at the box office

1992 Paid $12.5 million to lead all-star cast of *A Few Good Men,* which earns $102 million

1993 Stars in blockbuster hit *The Firm*, which earns more than $150 million; adopts Isabella Jane Kidman Cruise; directs *The Frightening Frammies*

1994 Takes on role of the evil vampire Lestat in *Interview with the Vampire*

1995 Adopts Connor Antony Kidman Cruise

1996 Makes *Mission: Impossible* with director Brian De Palma; *Mission: Impossible* makes more than $400 million to become one of the biggest moneymaking films of all time

1997 Nominated for second Academy Award for excellent performance as a sports agent in *Jerry Maguire*

1998 Works with Kidman and director Stanley Kubrick on the film *Eyes Wide Shut* in London

1999 *Eyes Wide Shut* expected to be released in March

FILMOGRAPHY

Endless Love, 1981 (directed by Franco Zeffirelli; 115 minutes). Costarring: Brooke Shields, Martin Hewitt, Shirley Knight, Don Murray, Richard Kiley, James Spader.

Taps, 1981 (directed by Harold Becker; 122 minutes). Costarring: George C. Scott, Timothy Hutton, Sean Penn, Ronny Cox, Brendan Ward.

Losin' It, 1983 (directed by Curtis Hanson; 100 minutes). Costarring: Shelley Long, Jackie Earle Haley, John Stockwell, John P. Navin Jr., Henry Darrow.

The Outsiders, 1983 (directed by Francis Ford Coppola; 91 minutes). Costarring: C. Thomas Howell, Matt Dillon, Ralph Macchio, Patrick Swayze, Rob Lowe, Diane Lane, Emilio Estevez, Tom Cruise, Leif Garrett, Tom Waits, Sofia Coppola.

Risky Business, 1983 (directed by Paul Brickman; 97 minutes). Costarring: Rebecca De Mornay, Curtis Armstrong, Bronson Pinchot, Raphael Sbarge, Richard Masur, Kevin Anderson.

All the Right Moves, 1983 (directed by Michael Chapman; 90 minutes). Costarring: Craig T. Nelson, Lea Thompson, Charles Cioffi, Paul Carafotes, Christopher Penn.

Legend, 1985 (directed by Ridley Scott; 94 minutes). Costarring Mia Sara, Tim Curry, David Bennent, Alice Playten, Billy Barty.

Top Gun, 1986 (directed by Tony Scott; 110 minutes). Costarring: Kelly McGillis, Val Kilmer, Anthony Edwards, Tom Skerritt, Michael Ironside, John Stockwell, Meg Ryan, Barry Tubb, Tim Robbins.

The Color of Money, 1987 (directed by Martin Scorsese; 119 minutes). Costarring: Paul Newman, Mary Elizabeth Mastrantonio, Helen Shaver, John Turturro, Forrest Whitaker, Iggy Pop.

Cocktail, 1988 (directed by Roger Donaldson; 100 minutes). Costarring: Bryan Brown, Elisabeth Shue, Lisa Banes, Kelly Lynch, Paul Benedict.

Rain Man, 1988 (directed by Barry Levinson; 140 minutes). Costarring: Dustin Hoffman, Valeria Golino, Jerry Molden, Jack Murdock, Michael D. Roberts.

Born on the Fourth of July, 1989 (directed by Oliver Stone; 144 minutes). Costarring: Willem Dafoe, Raymond J. Barry, Caroline Kava, Kyra Sedgwick, Bryan Larkin, Stephen Baldwin, Tom Berenger.

Days of Thunder, 1990 (directed by Tony Scott; 107 minutes). Costarring: Robert Duvall, Nicole Kidman, Randy Quaid, Cary Elwes, Michael Rooker, Fred Dalton Thompson.

Far and Away, 1991 (directed by Ron Howard; 140 minutes). Costarring: Nicole Kidman, Thomas Gibson, Robert Prosky, Cyril Cusack, Colm Meaney.

A Few Good Men, 1992 (directed by Rob Reiner; 138 minutes). Costarring: Jack Nicholson, Demi Moore, Kevin Bacon, Keifer Sutherland, Kevin Pollack.

The Firm, 1993 (directed by Sydney Pollack; 155 minutes). Costarring: Jeanne Tripplehorn, Gene Hackman, Hal Holbrook, Terry Kinney, Wilford Brimley, Ed Harris, Holly Hunter, David Strathairn, Gary Busey, Steven Hill.

Interview with the Vampire, 1994 (directed by Neil Jordan; 122 minutes). Costarring: Brad Pitt, Kirsten Dunst, Christian Slater, Antonio Banderas, Stephen Rea.

Mission: Impossible, 1996 (directed by Brian De Palma; 110 minutes). Costarring: Jon Voight, Emmanuelle Beart, Henry Czerny, Jean Reno, Ving Rhames, Kristin Scott-Thomas, Vanessa Redgrave, Emilio Estevez.

Jerry Maguire, 1997 (directed by Cameron Crowe; 138 minutes). Costarring: Cuba Gooding Jr., Renee Zellweger, Kelly Preston, Jerry O'Connell, Jay Mohr, Bonnie Hunt, Regina King, Jonathan Lipnicki, Glenn Frey, Eric Stoltz, Jann Wenner, Alexandra Wentworth.

FURTHER READING

Tom Cruise

Bach, Julie. *Tom Cruise: Reaching for the Stars*. Minneapolis: Abdo and Daughters Publishing, 1993.

Brown, Gene. *Movie Time*. New York: Macmillan, 1995.

Cawley, Janet. "Tom Cruise: His Life, His Loves, and His Mysterious New Movie." *A & E Biography Magazine*, October 1998.

Clarkson, Wensley. *Tom Cruise: Unauthorised*. London: United Publishers Group, 1994.

"Face-off: How Today's Heartthrobs Compare with Generations Past." *People,* November 17, 1997.

Martin, Mick, and Marsha Petersonn. *Video Movie Guide*. New York: Ballantine Books, 1993.

McNair, Jean. "Since Movie, Navy Recruits Are Lining Up." The Associated Press, June 26, 1986.

Sellers, Robert. *Tom Cruise*. London: Robert Hale, 1997.

Dyslexia and Reading Disorders

Connelly, Elizabeth Russell. *A World Upside Down and Backwards: Reading and Learning Disorders*. Philadelphia: Chelsea House Publishers, 1999.

Huston, Anne Marshall. *Understanding Dyslexia: A Practical Approach for Parents and Teachers*. Lanham, Md.: Madison Books, 1992.

Knox, Jean McBee. *Learning Disabilities*. Philadelphia: Chelsea House Publishers, 1989.

Nosek, Kathleen. *The Dyslexic Scholar.* Dallas: Taylor Publishing, 1995.

Osmond, John. *The Reality of Dyslexia.* Herndon, Va.: Cassell Academic, 1993.

Sargent, Dave, and Laura Tirella. *What Every Teacher & Parent Should Know About Dyslexia*. Prairie Grove, Ark.: Ozark Publishing, 1996.

Scientology

Atack, Jon. *A Piece of Blue Sky: Scientology, Dianetics and L. Ron Hubbard Exposed.* Secaucus, N.J.: Lyle Stuart, 1990.

Behar, Richard. "The Prophet and Profits of Scientology." *Forbes,* October 27, 1986.

Carassava, Anthee. "Court Rips Scientology." The Associated Press, January 18, 1997.

Hubbard, L. Ron. *Dianetics: The Modern Science of Mental Health.* Los Angeles: Bridge Publishers, 1995.

———. *Scientology: The Fundamentals of Thought.* Los Angeles: Bridge Publishers, 1997.

APPENDIX

ORGANIZATIONS THAT DEAL WITH DYSLEXIA AND OTHER LEARNING DISORDERS

American Academy of Child and Adolescent Psychiatry (AACAP)
3615 Wisconsin Ave., NW
Washington, DC 20016-3007
(202) 966-7300

American Speech-Language-Hearing Association (ASHA)
10801 Rockville Pike
Rockville, MD 20852
(301) 897-5700

Association on Higher Education and Disability (AHEAD)
P.O. Box 21192
Columbus, OH 43221-0192
(614) 488-4972

Canadian Mental Health Association (CMHA)
970 Lawrence Ave. West, Suite 205
Toronto, Ontario M6A 3B6, Canada
(416) 789-7957

**Council for Exceptional Children,
Eric Clearinghouse on Disabilities & Gifted Children**
1920 Association Drive
Reston, VA 22091
(800) 328-0272

Council for Learning Disabilities
P.O. Box 40303
Overland Park, KS 66204
(913) 492-8755

Gow School
Emery Road
South Wales, NY 14139
(716) 652-3450, (800) 724-0138

The International Dyslexia Association
8600 Lasalle Road
Chester Building, Suite 382
Baltimore, MD 21286
(410) 296-0232, (800) 222-3123

Kennedy Krieger Institute
707 North Broadway
Baltimore, MD 21205
(888) 554-2080

Learning Disabilities Association of America (LDAA)
4156 Library Road
Pittsburgh, PA 15234
(412) 341-1515, (412) 341-8077

Learning Disabilities Association of Canada (LDAC)
323 Chapel St., Suite 200
Ottawa, Ontario K1N 7Z2, Canada
(613) 238-5721

National Alliance for the Mentally Ill
Child and Adolescent Network (NAMI-CAN)
200 North Glebe Road, Suite 1015
Arlington, VA 22203-3754
(800) 950-NAMI

National Center for Learning Disabilities
381 Park Ave. South, Suite 1420
New York, NY 10016
(212) 545-7510

National Information Center for Children and Youth with Disabilities (NICHCY)
P.O. Box 1492
Washington, DC 20013
(800) 695-0285

Parents Educational Resource Center
1660 South Amphlett Boulevard, Suite 200
San Mateo, CA 94402-2508
(415) 655-2410

INDEX

PICTURE CREDITS

Phelan Powell wrote for her college newspaper in Boston and created a cartoon strip for the same. As a Coast Guard reservist, she worked in the public affairs office and dealt with press relations. Powell has worked as a daily correspondent for the *Michigan City News-Dispatch* and is the author of biographies on hockey star John LeClair, comedian John Candy, and the music group Hanson, as well as a book on unsolved crimes.

James Scott Brady serves on the board of trustees with the Center to Prevent Handgun Violence and is the Vice Chairman of the Brain Injury Foundation. Mr. Brady served as Assistant to the President and White House Press Secretary under President Ronald Reagan. He was severely injured in an assassination attempt on the president, but remained the White House Press Secretary until the end of the administration. Since leaving the White House, Mr. Brady has lobbied for stronger gun laws. In November 1993, President Bill Clinton signed the Brady Bill, a national law requiring a waiting period on handgun purchases and a background check on buyers.